Sunderland
Tramways To Busways

by

Matty Morrison

*The Carroll brothers – all Corporation drivers, left to right: Paddy, Bobby and John.
Below: Paddy Carroll meets Princess Diana.*

Acknowledgements

People whose names and photographs appear in this book have made a major contribution, without them the book would never have happened. There are, of course, some people who deserve special thanks for their donations of photographs from family albums and information that was known only to them. Many thanks to: Ian Alderson, Peter Bogan, Eleanor Brannigan, Frank Charlton, Betty Charlton, Tommy and Terry Derivan, Malcolm M. Fraser MBE, Carol Giles, Mrs Lesley Gillies, Sue Kirtley, John Lounds, Charlie Parnaby, Arthur Priest, Billy Smith, Tommy Smith, John T. Scott, Billy Tarvit, Kevin Taylor, Mr & Mrs Jimmy Temple, Doug Watson and Billy Youern.

I would also like to thank the following organisations for their help with this publication: Nexus, Sunderland Library, Sunderland Echo and Stagecoach Busways.

Previous page: Support strike action! 16th October 1974.

Back cover: Wartime conductress Annie Jukes née Morrison, 1944. Like many women of the time, Annie helped the war effort by going to work for the Corporation. Unlike many of her colleagues Annie never got the chance to go permanent, or, take up the chance of driving, because she chose to look after her husband, after his return from war. And she did just that with great success.

Introduction

Billy Rowe around 1939 on his way to the 'real' war.

Of all of the many great industries that have arisen in and around Sunderland none have been documented more than the Sunderland Transport Corporation Department. The Hansom cab from the earliest beginnings, the tram cars and, later, the buses were the vehicles of the Department and many books have been written documenting the technical details of the undertaking, but what of the most important commodity, THE PEOPLE. The employees, the innovators, and the travelling public all of whom not only developed the transport undertakings but determined the development and the growth of what is now a city.

There must be many stories told in the other industries, such as the shipyards and the mines, but none could compare with the romance and family traditions of the Corporation. The close comradeship of the 'crews' not only among themselves but the affinities with their vehicles be they trams or buses.

I intend to illustrate in this book in the best possible and true light the human involvement in the building of the Transport undertaking over the past 100 years – from the 1870s until the demise of the Corporation in 1974. Sadly in doing so I will inadvertently omit to mention someone who will have been important and include someone who some of the readers will think were not so important and should not have been included. May I, in advance, apologise and assure the reader that all inclusions will be true to the best of my knowledge.

Like most young boys of the time, the late 1940s, I wanted to be a soldier, but I wanted to be a soldier like Mr Rowe. Mr Rowe, or Billy Rowe as he became known to me many years later, was different to other soldiers because of his uniform. Unlike others his uniform was dark blue and had shiny buttons, and I could see him most times of the day, and almost everyday. I used to march behind him, in time, down Ward Street in Hendon where we lived, and watch him board his 'tank' and go off to 'war'. Many years later I found out that Billy's 'tank' was a tramcar and that he, after returning from his service in the Army, was now going to war for Sunderland Corporation Transport Department. I am certain that that is where my original fascination with the

A tram at Villette Road terminus – My first paid job around 1949.

Corporation began. I did meet Billy for a short time around 1949-50 when I used to take a couple of days off school and go to Villette Road terminus and wait for the trams to turn up. I then used to board the tram and push the backs of the seats the opposite way so that the passengers were facing the right way to go back to the town. I was then sometimes 'paid' for my work by the conductors by the princely sum of one halfpenny. After some hours those halfpennies amounted to quite a bit for which my mother was most grateful.

Twenty years, and many jobs later, including my own military service, I arrived at the Wheatsheaf to begin 27 years service with the Corporation, and, there I met my 'old soldier' again.

Sadly Billy passed away on 17th November 2000, aged 89 years.

Above: Master Matty Morrison, aged 5, ready to start work on the trams at halfpenny a time.

Right: That's me in uniform around 1995.

It is hard to imagine, standing here in the December cold and rain, without shelter, who is to blame for the bus that should have turned up 20 minutes ago? Who decided that I would need to use public transport to travel to and return from work? Would my life have been easier with 'Shank's pony?' Well let us look back and see what kind of people decreed that this should be so.

The gentry were travelling in their private coaches from very early in the eighteenth century, and the ordinary folk were either pedestrians or were moving around on horseback, There were inter town or county transport for long distance travel but nothing for the locals to use around the towns or cities. Such a vehicle came along in 1834 – a 'cab' that was small enough for the towns but large enough to carry two passengers. It, the cab, was pulled by one horse, unlike the coaches that were pulled by two or four or six horses. So here is

Hansom Cab around 1850.

the culprit who began encouraging ordinary people to leave 'Shank's pony' and travel around with ease. The person who introduced the cab was Joseph Aloysius Hansom (1803-1882), and that is why forever the individual cab would become known as the Hansom Cab.

The Hansom Cab and the domestic coaches would have an historical effect on the lives of people nationally. In London, Jack the Ripper was reportedly to have used the Hansom Cab for his dastardly deeds, while Dick Turpin the highwayman, certainly took advantage of the inter city coaches to enhance his income. However, no such exciting events took place in Sunderland until maybe 12th June 1879, when the first tram of the Sunderland Tramway Company crossed the bridge over the River Wear into Fawcett Street and into a roadblock of Hansom Cabs.

The Sunderland Tramways Company had been in operation for approximately a year, operating on the north side of the river. The Company had, with the assistance of Sir Hedworth Williamson, applied for and gained permission through an Act of Parliament to set up a permanent tramway for the use of the public in Sunderland. The first directors of the Company were as follows: Captain J.M. Gillies (chairman), Sir William Monclare, E.T. Gourley and Sir John Humphrey. The manager was George A. Berry. Because of their initial success the Company decided quite early on to extend operations south of the river, and so began the fracas on the 12th June 1879.

Sunderland Cabmen 1880

James Bell, aged 26	58 Northumberland Street
John Moffet, aged 35	52 Northumberland Street
Chas A. Wilkinson, aged 25	48 Northumberland Street
Sarah A. Wilkinson, aged 24	48 Northumberland Street
Mary Peacock, aged 50	37 Northumberland Street
Joseph Peacock, aged 23	37 Northumberland Street
William Peacock, aged 21	37 Northumberland Street
William Vazey, aged 28	22 Northumberland Street
Fortune Wilkinson, aged 50	22 Northumberland Street
Cuthbert Wilkinson, aged 17	22 Northumberland Street
Thos A. Wilkinson, aged 27	22 Northumberland Street
James A. Anderson, aged 26	13 Northumberland Street
Fred J. Wilkinson, aged 29	14 South Street
John Peacock, aged 26	22 West Street
William J. Davison, aged 33	11 Vine Place
Thomas Swan, aged 28	29 Cousin Street
Thomas Dunn, aged 23	50 Hendon Street
James Proctor, aged 23	6 Clarke Terrace
Robert H. Lee, aged 20	56 Moor Street
William Martin, aged 22	30 Pemberton Street
Alfred Gregson	

Above and facing page: Opposing sides in the fight of Fawcett Street around 1879.

First converted single to double deck horse drawn tram about to make its first journey from Roker to Monkwearmouth in 1880.

One of the first horse drawn trams similar to the one driven by Thomas E. Carter over the Sunderland Bridge in 1879.

Sunderland Tramways Company 1880

Directors – J.M. Giles, William Monclare, F.T. Gourley, John Humphrey. Manager – Mr A. Berry

Andrew Atkinson, aged 27, Driver	141 Church Street
Stephen Harding, aged 20, Driver	141 Church Street
F. Romans, aged 21, Driver	207 Roker Avenue
J. Allison, aged 22 , Driver	207 Roker Avenue
James Coulson, aged 18, Driver	207 Roker Avenue
William Story, aged 51, Driver	20 Hedworth Street
William Martin, aged 18, Driver	10 Pemberton Street
Thomas Youman , Driver	
Titus Richards, Stableman	
Thomas Carter, Driver	Northumberland St.
John Allan, aged 11, Conductor	14 Adalaide Place
Charles Allan, aged 15, Conductor	14 Adalaide Place
George E. Short, aged 20, Conductor	Ferry Landing
Alfred E. Scott, aged 20, Conductor	3 Fenwick Street
Frederick H. Smith, aged 15, Conductor	141 Church Street
John T. Hailes, aged 13, Conductor	47 Southwick Terrace
John Latimer, aged 17, Conductor	7 Blue Bell Yard
Thomas Harper, aged 18, Conductor	16 Wilson Street
John T.B. Ward, aged 15, Conductor	16 Wilson Street
Henry Convery, aged 17, Conductor	7 Stobbard Street
Henry Molloy, aged 40, Horse Keeper	133 Church Street
Geo. W. Molloy, aged 19, Horse Keeper	133 Church Street
Thomas W Thornton, aged 35, Repairer	192 Roker Ave
Thomas Watson, aged 47, Labourer	55 Northumberland St.
John Watson, aged 11, Labourer	55 Northumberland St.
Henry Molloy, aged 16, Road Boy	133 Church Street
Thomas Sweeting, Yard Boy	

Horse drawn tram in Fawcett Street with Mackie's Corner in the background.

The incident, which was heated, was attended by the police, and was later taken before the courts, where the full story emerged.

Mr Thomas E. Carter aged 30, of 56 Northumberland Street, the first tram driver to cross the Sunderland Bridge was taking his tramcar, driven by one horse, down Fawcett Street when he encountered a number of Hansom Cabs blocking his way. He made an attempt to move through the blockade, when he was physically attacked by two men from the crowd of cabmen that were assembled. The two men, Alfred Gregson and William Martin, were charged with assault. Their reason for attacking Mr Carter was that he provoked them by driving the tramcar into an area where they earned their living and that the Tramways Company had failed to notify all the cabmen that they, the Company, intended to operate horse drawn tramcars south of the river. The court also informed the cabmen that the Company should have informed

At Southwick Terminus 1900.

them that the Company had been acting though permission of an Act of Parliament and that because of such an omission to inform the cabmen, they, the cabmen, had acted in ignorance. The representative for the Company agreed with the court that they had been negligent and so agreed with the bench that the assault case against the two cabmen should be dismissed.

While I was researching this case a number of interesting points came to light. The fact Mr William Martin, one of the cabmen involved in the attack on Mr Thomas Carter, later became a senior tramcar driver. There were about 20 or so Hansom Cabs in operation in Sunderland at the time, supposedly on individual licence, how interesting that a family called Wilkinson, all of Northumberland Street, had a number of cabs and people involved in 'public transport'. Along with the Wilkinsons and, still in Northumberland Street, were the Peacocks who also had a number of cabs. It must have been more than a little difficult for someone else who was also living in Northumberland Street, and that was Mr Thomas E. Carter, the tram driver who was involved in the first instance with the cabmen in Fawcett Street. Might the provocation that the cabmen had indicated in their court case have had its beginnings a little closer to home.

First of the electric trams on show in Ryhope Road in August 1900 and on the Sunderland Bridge (below).

In 1882 Mr William Morrison along with Mr Frederick J. Farrell were the managers of the Tramways Company and, judging by the financial statements of the period (1879-1900), they were responsible for putting the Company on a sound footing. However, there were other aspects of their joint responsibilities that were not so favourable. Both managers at various times were invited by the criminal courts of the day, to attend a number of their sessions in regard to the cruelty of the Company toward their horses.

Thomas Sweeting, a stable boy, in the employ of the Tramways Company, was charged with cruelty to a draw horse. After some discussion Mr Morrison admitted that the boy was acting under his orders. The court agreed and fined Mr Morrison 20 shillings. The spokesman for the bench also said he understood that

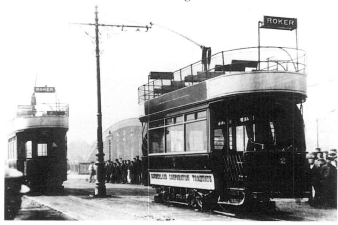

another offence against the same horse was committed on the 25th of the same month, and that he held Mr Morrison responsible. Mr Morrison agreed with the bench, and was fined again, On a third occasion, on the 27th, Titus Richards a stableman for Tramways was charged with cruelty, along with William Morrison. This time, however, both men were held responsible. Morrison was fined £5 and Richards was fined 5 shillings. The chairman of the bench went on to warn Titus Richards, that although he was just a servant of Tramways, should he be brought in front of the bench again, he would not only be fined, but he would be sent to Durham.

Many court cases involving cruelty to the horses of the Tramways Company stemmed from the steep inclines on the routes that the horses were expected to pull their tramcars. One such case was regarding a prosecution brought against James Garroway, tram driver, Mr Morrison manager and James Knight horse keeper. On Monday 8th January 1883 at 3.50 pm Garroway was driving a tramcar, which was being pulled by two horses up the incline at Cornhill, Southwick. Because of wounds on both horses on all of their legs they were having great difficulty in taking the tram up the incline. Garroway was seen to whip the horses repeatedly by a passer-by, fortunately for the horses the passer-by was none other than inspector Nichols of the R.S.P.C.A. who instructed the driver to stop, which the driver did immediately. The inspector then ordered the horses to be returned to the depot at the Wheatsheaf, where upon arrival they were met by the manager Mr Morrison who was to make the comment, 'something wrong again inspector', After being told of the problem with the condition of the horses, Mr Knight interrupted and informed that Mr Morrison knew of their condition before they went out of the depot. On Wednesday 10th January Mr W. Hunter, a veterinary surgeon, went to the depot but was refused entry by Mr Knight. After some time the party were able to gain access and inspect the horses, and forthwith declared them unfit to work, and pointed out that they, the horses had been in that condition for some time. Mr Morrison in defence told the court that he had instructions for his horse dealers, such as Mr Knight, that if any of the horses were not well at any time, that they should be replaced with the spare horses which were kept in the depot for just that purpose. The court heard from witnesses that while the instructions of Mr Morrison were known, those instructions were not posted anywhere in the depot.

The court instructed Mr Morrison to do so immediately. Garroway, the driver was ordered to pay costs, while Morrison and Knight were fined 10 shillings each, and ordered to pay costs.

The magistrates made comment that they were aware of the increasing number of complaints against the Tramways Company, and that these complaints must decrease dramatically or someone, very soon would be looking at a custodial sentence.

It is noticeable that there were not so many cases, of a similar nature as the previous case that involved the Tramways Company. That is not to say that there were not any.

Mr Morrison may have had some troubles involving the courts at one time or another, but what we can be assured of is that he and the Tramways staff kept the Company in profit for the rest of Mr Morrison's time until he left in 1901.

The Company, between 1883 and 1895, continued to progress financially and expand their tramway tracks throughout the town. Nothing dramatic occurred until 1895 when, after many meetings within the committees of the Town Council, it was decided that the Corporation would not renew the Transport Lease to the Tramways Company when it expired, and that they, the Corporation were considering operating the franchise themselves, and finally on the 26th March 1900 the purchase of the Tramways went ahead at a cost of £35,000. The Wheatsheaf tram depot was to be taken over along with all the rolling stock at the same time of the purchase.

On the 26th July 1900 the first two electric tramcars were delivered, and later, another six were delivered, and finally, after the first two cars were shown to the very interested public of Sunderland, and after some inclement weather, the first electric tramcar ran in service on the 15th August 1900, an 11-year-old girl hastily becoming the first passenger.

Harry England, first Electric Tramways Manager.

With the coming of the electric trams, the aroma of straw covered lines, the smell of sweating horses, the excitement of young children running to catch a free ride on the back of the tram would now, with sadness, pass into history. On the 23rd March 1901 the last 32 horses were sold by auction.

The electrically operated tram era brought with it the need for a new specialist management team.

On 30th March 1900, Mr F.C. Snell, who was the Borough Electrical Engineer, was appointed the first Tramways General Manager along with Mr R.S. Rounthwaite to develop the new Electric Tramways system. William Morrison was to carry on with the day-to-day running of Tramways until he was replaced by Mr Harry England. Mr England only stayed for two years, before becoming manager of West Riding Tramways. The next General Manager was to be Mr Archibald Robert Dayson who was already Traffic Manager under Mr Snell, he would take up the new post on Mr Snell's resignation in 1907. Mr Dayson was to take the Tramways into the future by his modernisation of the trams their routes and, of course,

Archibald Dayson (in the second row in the grey suit) with the staff of the Hylton Road Depot, 1905.

his unique man-management.

Hylton Road Depot, at the junction of Trimdon Street, Farringdon Row and Hylton Road, opened 30th September 1903. It was officially opened by Councillor Summerbell, Chairman of the Tramways Committee. The depot was big enough to accommodate 50 trams, a paint shop,

Hylton Road Depot before its opening in 1903.

and blacksmiths. The cottage, already attached at the side of the building was used as offices, and years later became a caretaker's home. Later the depot would build Sunderland's own trams, and later still it would be converted to a bus depot.

Decorated tram – celebrating the signing of the Vereeniging Treaty ending the Boer War on 31st May 1902 – outside of Wheatsheaf Depot.

Percy Seymour
Driver
1940s-1970s

Charlie Blyth
Driver
1940s-1970s

Tommy Skinner
Conductor
1940s-1970s

Gordon Smith
Driver
1950s-1970s

Bobby Martin
Driver
1940s-1970s

David Bloomfield
Inspector
1960s-1970s

Albert Maxted
Conductor
1940s-1970s

Ivy Coates
Conductress
1940s-1970s

Jacky Thompson
Conductor
1940s-1970s

Joan Jacobs
Conductress
1950s-1970s

When the Sunderland Corporation took over the Tramways Company in 1900, they also acquired the Wheatsheaf Depot, which was reconstructed from stables to accommodate 50 trams, while a temporary office block was built in Fawcett Street, near the old Town Hall. A new Wheatsheaf Depot would be purpose-built and would open in 1905. The new building would stand on the same ground as the old depot, but would contain many new features, such as better facilities for the transport staff, and the new engineering workforce. The engineers would have a number of 'pits' available to them so that they could carry out work underneath the trams, and have easier access to the bogies, where most of the general maintenance was necessary. The transport staff, mainly conductors, would be provided with custom built 'cash cabins', where they could total up their work for the day, in peace. It was common practice for drivers and conductors, while on the road, to leave their tea-cans downstairs, so that one of their colleagues could see that it was filled, and brought back downstairs so the owners of the tea-can could have a cuppa' while still on duty at the outside terminus.

Even though the new Wheatsheaf would provide better canteen facilities for the staff, the tea-can practice, would continue for many years into the future. So much so that one of the favourite sayings by the public, to the drivers and conductors, would be 'been tea'ing at the terminus, is that why you're late? For the engineers, the use of canteens was something really unique, never had such facilities been afforded to them before, and this particular amenity was to copied by other industries, such as the shipyards and the mines. Never was it known in any company before but the Wheatsheaf was to also have a rest room provided for the staff – how modern. The temporary offices in Fawcett Street was where the staff were to collect their wages, so *temporary* were the offices, that staff were still collecting their wages there until a completely new Wheatsheaf office block was built in 1967.

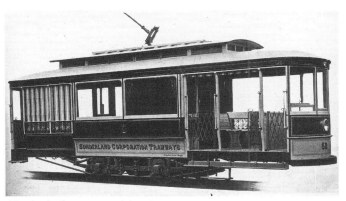

Single deck tram combination.

The new Wheatsheaf office block around 1905.

Track laying workmen outside Wheatsheaf Depot around 1901. It's not known whether the men are Tramways employees or contract workers, but I'm sure that they would take full advantage of the facilities in the depot. That's of course, provided the Tramways Company would allow such an action.

SUNDERLAND CORPORATION TRAMWAYS.

HYLTON ROAD DEPOT.

NOTICE.
SMOKING
DURING WORK HOURS

Smoking will be allowed in all these Works, except the Joiners' Shop and the Stores, between the hours of 9-0 a.m. and 11 a.m. and 1-0 p.m. and 3-0 p.m.

It is hoped that the men will appreciate this concession and loyally abide by the times above stated, also that they will exercise every care as to the throwing about of matches and smouldering cigarette ends and tobacco, in order that the risk of fire may be reduced to a minimum.

A. R. DAYSON.
General Manager and Engineer.

You could smoke inside the Hylton Road Depot around 1905.

Children being taken on a ride on the new electric trams around 1905.

Although 4 years had passed and 40 new trams had been added to the Tramways fleet, since the take over by the Corporation, not a lot of improvements or modifications that were obvious, had been made to the trams themselves. That observation does not seem to affect the excitement of the children in the picture, they appear as though they could not care less what the tram looks like as long as they can get aboard for what is probably their first ride on a tram. There are four trams in the photograph, giving me the impression that the outing is an organised school trip, probably for children from schools in Fulwell and Monkwearmouth areas. The trams are standing at Sea View Road, what was then the terminus end of journey for the town to Fulwell route.

It is sad to reflect that, although, all the children appear to be attired in their Sunday best, those in the

Alderman George New, longest serving Transport Committee Chairman 1906-1929.

foreground are short of footwear, apparently commonplace in 1905.

In 1906 Alderman George New was to take over as Chairman of the Council's Transport Committee. He was to serve as one of the longest serving Chairman for 23 years, and so he was to preside over many of the changes that were to take place in the Corporation.

Tram driver John Metcalf 1900-1934 with his conductor.

Joe Matthews
Driver
1940s-1970s

Kenny Blackburn
Conductor/Driver
1957-1963

Cedric Carter
Driver
1940s-1970s

John Eager
Driver
1971-1998

Keith Barker
Driver
1968-Today

Dennis Stothard
Driver
1970-Today

Alan Senior
Driver
1970-1995

Bobby Park
Driver
1965-Today

John Robinson
Driver
1970-1995

Norman Gair
Driver
1969-1996

One of the longest serving members of the office staff was Miss Edith Kirton. Miss Kirton worked in the ticket office for 41 years, and was most pleased when the sale of tickets became automated with the new 'set-right' machine. Edith was also a keen amateur actress and took part in many productions that were performed for the staff, including 'Androcles and the Lion' and ' A Christmas Carol'. Miss Kirton retired at the end of October 1955. Sadly after only 14 years of well-earned retirement Miss Kirton passed away in March 1969 aged 73 years.

General office staff, circa 1950. Back, left to right: Ruth Turnbull, Miss Heskitt, Mrs Craggs, Margaret Shaw. Front: Margaret Ann Holmes, Annie Ramsey and Edith Kirton.

In 1916 one of the most significant and, probably one of the saddest incidents, took place right on the doorstep of the Wheatsheaf Tramway Offices. On 1st April of that year, a Zeppelin dropped a bomb on Sunderland making a direct hit on a tramcar. The Tramcar was fleet No. 10 and the conductor was one Margaret Ann Holmes. The regulations regarding staff in relation to the safety of passengers was such, that the conductor would remain with the tram when air raid warnings were sounded. Miss Holmes carried out her duties and in doing so was seriously injured; having her right leg badly damaged. Having spent some months in hospital, she returned to work in the Tramways offices, until her retirement in 1950. Miss Holmes continued to live with her niece in Inverness Street, Fulwell, until, sadly she passed away on 11th March 1986, aged 91. In the same incident an inspector was killed, unfortunately I do not have the inspector's name. There was also another 22 people killed along with 105 people injured during the raid.

Margaret Ann Holmes in 1916 before the Zeppelin bomb dropped on the Wheatsheaf.

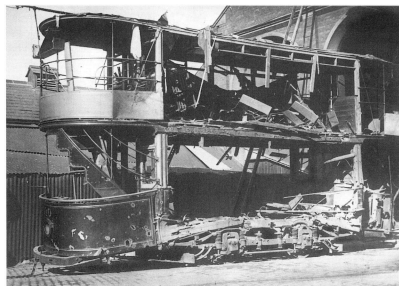

Above: Tram No. 10 after the bomb on 1st April 1916.

Right: Tram No. 10, replacement for the bombed tram.

Above: Miss Jean Newton, World War One conductress, badge No. 331.

Right: Mrs May Rich née Ambler, tram conductress/driver, around 1916. As a 16-year-old she became the youngest tram driver.

World War One conductress Liza Smith.

Born 9th December 1900 Miss May Ambler was to become the youngest tram driver at the age of just sixteen. She was later to marry and become Mrs May Rich. She died on her 85th birthday.

William Proudfoot retired in June 1955 after 49 years service – 24 years as a tram driver and then as motor inspector. Like most tram drivers he began working as a points boy at the age of 17 and he retired as traffic inspector which he had held for two years. Mr Proudfoot was famous for driving his tram back to the Wheatsheaf Depot after it was involved in an accident, it may sound a little trivial, but the body of the tram was hanging off the trolleys, and was in real danger of catching fire. If it were not for Mr Proudfoot's quick thinking things could have been a little more serious for the public. William Proudfoot's parting words at his retirement presentation were 'and I suppose that the bus will be the future, but it is with fondness that I will remember my working life with the tram car in mind.'

During both World Wars lots of women were to take on jobs while their men were away in the trenches above are just a few.

Arthur Smith
Engineer
1970s

Doug Summerside
Engineer
1970s

Alan Tomlin
Engineer
1970s

William Wallace
Engineer
1970s

Charlie Bowey
Engineer
1970s

Keith Edmunds
Engineer
1970s

Jimmy Hanson
Engineer
1970s

Brian Kemp
Conductor/Engineer
1970s

Kenny Little
Engineer
1970s

Alan Middleton
Engineer
1970s

Born in 1896, and starting work around the same time as May Amber, and probably one of her friends, was Miss Annie Goodhall. Annie was also a conductress that would take the opportunity of becoming one of the first five lady drivers in World War One, albeit, like many of the young soldiers of the day, she would lie about her age. Annie was one of the first ladies to take up the challenge of conducting on the trams, and she was also one of the last to leave after the war was over.

Some of her memories of the war were recalled during an interview in 1969. Annie had only been driving for a few months but, she recalled the time when the Zeppelins were dropping bombs in Fawcett Street in 1916, and in pitch darkness, she had to guide her passengers to safety in a piano shop.

Being a Hendon girl Annie can recall having to run from home most mornings, down to the Wheatsheaf Depot, so that she would be on time to go back to Grangetown to pick up the munitions workers at 3.30 in the morning. Conscientious to the

Above: Annie Hogg as Annie Goodhall, third from the left in the rear. Miss Jean Newton first left front row.

Left: Annie Goodhall with points boy in 1918.

Right: Annie Hogg on her retirement. October 1969.

last, as the driver of the tram, she would put her foot down to ensure that the men would arrive on time.

It is not known for certain if Annie was to marry another Corporation employee, but she did marry her husband, Wilfred Hogg, in St Mary's RC Church, in 1923. Wilfred was still alive when Annie gave her interview in 1969, he was 73 years old. She began her reminisces when she came across an old photograph of herself and her conductress of a few years, Mrs E. Harrison. The photograph was taken outside of the Wheatsheaf just before the end of the war.

The 12th August 1959 saw the end of an era in local shipping when the ferry service across the Wear ceased. No longer would we see the transporting of great hordes of workmen from one side of the river to the other. Corporation buses would now provide the means to take people to work instead of the ferry.

It is interesting to note that the route the new bus service was to take would lengthen the journey that the ferry used to take by nine times the distance.

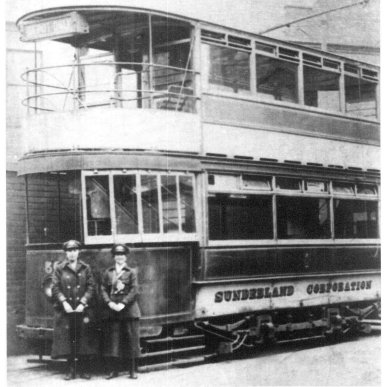

Annie Hogg, driver (left) and Mrs E. Harrison, conductress, 1918.

Above: Tram No. 63 opposite the Transport Club in North Bridge Street in 1945.

Right: Conductor John Charlton killed in action in 1942.

Below: William Charlton, tram driver.

William Charlton began with the Corporation as most new employees as a points boy in 1915 and then graduated through the ranks to emerge as a tram driver. He had served with the Durham Light Infantry during the Great War as a driver, and he was happy to continue driving when he was demobbed. William, for various reasons, would carry out many other jobs, including that of track man, and later, when the trams stopped running, as a painter's labourer. Like many other tram drivers he was most upset at the demise of the trams, and at his retirement, on 28th April 1961, he made his feelings known. 'No I don't think the buses do a good job' he said 'Buses are too expensive to run, with their high taxes, and cost of fuel, and they don't carry as many passengers as the trams did'. Chairman of the Transport Committee, Mr Thomas Atkinson, presented William with a gold watch, after 47 years service, and he also received a wallet and notes, collected from 70 of his workmates at the Wheatsheaf Depot. William was to marry and produce four sons. With his wife and his children he liked nothing more than taking walks in the country and, taking picnics. One of his sons, John Charlton, was to become a conductor for the Corporation in 1941. A year later John was conscripted into the services, and was to eventually join the Royal Air Force as a fighter pilot. He was over St Malo in France, in July 1944, when he was shot down and killed. He is at rest in a military graveyard in Dinard, France. He was just 22 years of age when he left his widow Margaret Hilda Charlton née Wilcox, who he met when she was a conductress with the Corporation. William Charlton's other son, Frank, although he never worked in the transport area, must have caught the bug from his father and brother, because he became an enthusiast on trams. He still continues today in the same vane, collecting photographs and artefacts about the Corporation. William Charlton passed away on 25th November 1972.

Terry Tye
Driver
1968-Today

Billy Youern
Driver
1969-1996

George Gair
Driver
1940-1962

Gordon Palmer
Driver
1971-Today

Peter Moore
Driver
1973-Today

Keith Pardey
Driver
1972-1997

Micky Paterson
Conductor/Driver
1966-Today

John Kenny
Conductor/Driver
1964-Today

Freddie Cooper
Driver
1971-1998

Alan Dobson
Driver
1973-Today

Mr Carney retires, circa 1952. Left to right: Inspector Jack Roberts, George Carney, Stanley Finkle and Councillor Atkinson.

Tram No. 51 – the water carrier.

Jack Roberts was to retire in September 1959 as Chief Inspector after 40 years service, having began with the Corporation in 1919. Jack, like most before him, began working as a points boy, but I wonder if he entertained the fair sex in the hide out at the corner of Fawcett Street, as some of the previous points boys. Innocently keeping the young ladies on the side of the Corporation. After coming through the period as a conductor, he was to become a driver. One of his favourite jobs at this time was to drive the 'water carrier' – Tram 51 – which had been in service since 1901, carrying 600 gallons of water. It had been specially built for cleaning the tram tracks from various kinds of dirt, for although the horse drawn trams had disappeared, there were still a number of horses around, leaving plenty of stuff for the gardens. All kinds of dirt had to be removed from the tracks, especially where there were inclines, because the tram wheels would not rotate on slippery lines. All trams, because of that problem, would carry a bag of sand. The water carrier was rebuilt in 1907 to carry 1,800 gallons, unique to Sunderland, this enabled the tracks to be cleaned further a field, because of the expanding routes and services. The fleet No. 51 was to be used again in 1932, for a new centre entrance tram, when the water carrier was disposed of in December of that year. Jack Roberts, however, was to be promoted to an inspector, and then on to Chief, he was known as a strict disciplinarian but was also fair. He had other more pleasant duties to perform such as presenting retiring employees with gifts and expressing the company's gratitude for their services. One of these presentations was to George Carney, cashier (above right).

With Jack Roberts there is some controversy over his real claim to fame as the driver of the official last tram. Some people say that Jack was on the last tram – Tram 86 – for the official photograph, but left the tram to blow the whistle to allow the procession of all the last trams to move off. As there is no explanation as to where Mr Roberts went after, and although there is no proof, I am inclined to believe that Jack Roberts, along with J.J. Glendenning the conductor, were the last official crew on the last tram in Sunderland.

Jack Roberts, conductor/tram driver/bus driver and Chief Inspector, 1919-Sept 1959.

Points boys hide out in Fawcett Street sometime before 1952.

Mr Stan Finkle came to work for the Corporation in 1908 as an office junior, through sheer hard work he progressed to become manager in 1949, having been involved on the financial side of the business. Mr Finkle was very interested in the welfare of other employees and was the first secretary of the Benevolent Fund which was set up in 1923, the fund still continues to this day. He continued his interest in people by carrying out his governorship of Monkwearmouth Hospital for over 20 years. Mr Finkle retired in 1953 and enjoyed 17 years of retirement until regretfully he passed away on 21st January 1970. The staff of the department will miss him and give thanks that Mr Finkle gave of his best on their behalf.

Stanley Finkle, manager, 1952.

With very early starting times for the staff of both Tramways and Busways, after a late night socialising, sometimes an excuse would be needed to have a lie in. One of the most unusual I have ever come across was from the wife of Johnny Lowden, tram driver. A keen motor cyclist, Johnny, was involved in an accident as a young boy, and he lost a leg. Being the kind of strong minded man that he was, he never let it effect his life too much, and he just got on with his handicap. He managed quiet well as a tram driver. Worked very hard, but, should he need a lie in, and he only used the excuse twice, his wife would run to the phone box in Hendon where they lived, and say that Johnny had snapped the leather strap on his leg, and didn't have a spare, and so was unable to come in today. After the demise of the trams, because of his handicap, Johnny was unable to go bus driving so he became the telephonist. Johnny died of a heart attack while in this job, at a very young age.

Conductor Bob Richardson (left) and his driver unknown.

Ray Ford
Driver
1963-1995

Percy Latham
Driver
1940s-1970s

Jimmy Kerr
Driver
1940s-1970s

Dicky Reed
Driver
1972-1997

'Hoss' Hutchinson
Driver
1970-1988

Tommy Fielding
Conductor/Driver
1952-1986

Billy Robinson
Conductor/Driver
1959-1982

Ralph Mills
Driver
1971-1979

Kenny Butler
Driver
1969-1978

Vince Storey
Driver
1971-1999

The name of the Department was changed in 1937, from Sunderland Corporation Tramways to Sunderland Corporation Transport. Already in 1939 the bus fleet was making inroads into the tram routes and at the outbreak of the Second World War the size of the bus fleet was, 14 single-deckers, 32 double-deckers and two tram-o-cars. The change to the staff, as in 1900 with the change over from horses to electric trams, must have been just as traumatic. Training tram drivers to be bus drivers must have been a nightmare. Many of the staff were not prepared to take on the task, so they either resigned, or went into the depot as handymen. I must take this opportunity to inform readers that during the war years that all employees carried out their duties in typical true English fashion, and honourably fulfilled their commitments, and emerged with pride and well earned dignity.

It appears that the argument of who was the last driver of tram number 86, the official last tram in Sunderland, is to carry on. After further investigation it has come to light that on 1st October 1954, that Roger Tongs Pickering was the driver to take 86 tram on its last journey round the town. Once again I have no proof that this is so, but it was reported at the time of Rogers death in November 1962, that this event took place. Roger, however, did take one of the trams on its last journey along the sea front on 1st January 1954. He was accompanied by his conductress, Sally Rooks, along with their one and only passenger, Malcolm M. Fraser MBE. That is where the proof of this action came from. Malcolm is one of the leading authorities on

Tram No. 84 one of the Sunderland-built trams at Hylton Road Depot in 1933.

transport and is well known throughout the transport world. Roger Pickering was born in 1889, orphaned at an early age, he began working for Tramways in 1905 at the age of 15. He became a points boy and then a tram driver, and he was to complete 49 years service, retiring in 1954. Roger was a widower, but he was to leave a son Roger, who became a sergeant in the Royal Air Force, I wonder if Roger Jnr could shed some light on these facts.

Above: Roger Tongs Pickering, last tram driver, along the sea front, 3rd January 1954.

Right: Jim 'Bluey' Millington, conductor, December 1952.

Left: Having a fag at Seaburn terminus, June 1949. Driver Tommy Doyle (left) and his conductor John Hunter.

Charles Albert Hopkins, 'Charlie' as he was affectionately to be known by the staff, arrived from Wigan Corporation to take over the mantle as General Manager on 1st May 1929. He gave of his best to ensure that the trams of the day would succeed by modernising the system, and through his efforts, the Sunderland trams were to become renowned throughout the country. In one of his first reports to the Transport Committee in August 1929, he surprised everyone with his choice of three options regarding the way forward for the transport in Sunderland. The options were:

1. To replace the trams with motor buses.
2. To replace the trams with Trolley buses.
3. To retain and modernise the tramway system.

Charles A. Hopkins, manager 1929, died 16th October 1948.

When they chose option 3, it meant a great deal of relief, not only to the Committee, but, to the staff of the Corporation. He endorsed his choice of options with this speech to the Committee: 'Here in Sunderland the local geography is such as to make ideal tramway routes, it is my belief that for the general transport conditions of Sunderland the tramcar is the ideal vehicle best suited for the purpose.' From this recommendation the tramcar would be safe for another 25 years. Despite the offer of a higher salary, Mr Hopkins was to turn down an offer from Blackpool in 1932, and continued his loyal service until his death, aged 62, in 1948. One of the best and well thought of managers by both management and staff would be sadly missed.

The idea of supplementing the tram service with one or two buses began to take place in 1927, basically to operate on the Docks service where the trams were running at a loss. In February 1928 buses began to operate around the Docks and up High Street, but the service was ran on behalf of the Corporation by the Northern General Transport Company, as the Corporation, although they had ordered the buses, never had the vehicles to operate the licence.

No. 16 bus one of the first single decks bought in 1929.

Grahame Gibbon
Coach Builder
1972-Today

Paul Griffiths
Coach Builder
1970-Today

Johnny Jobling
Fitter
1963-1998

Eddie Pratt
Fitter
1956-1996

Alan Scott
Coach Builder
1968-Today

Joe Robins
Engineer
1971-Today

Malcolm Gough
Engineer
1970s

Bob Hancil
Engineer
1970s

Billy Bell
Depot Foreman
1940s-1970s

Davy Mallaburn
Engineer
1965-Today

In 1931 the Corporation's football team must have thought all their Christmas's had come at once. About to start as a conductor was a retired Sunderland AFC footballer, James Leslie Temple. Jimmy had began his football career with Gateshead in 1926, before playing for Sunderland. He then went on to play for Fulham

Jimmy Temple, points boy/tram/bus driver, and his wife Rose conductress.

before retiring from professional football and joining the Corporation. Jimmy, in his early days was renowned for his speed and was regarded as one of the North's fastest runners. Being conscripted for the Second World War, Jimmy served with the Army, and then returned to the Corporation where he continued his football, playing many times for the team. Fathering three sons, Jimmy Jnr, Arthur and Brian, he not only ensured that his family name would survive, but, that the tradition of Temples working in transport would continue. Jimmy Jnr, as a driver, and Arthur as storekeeper, would both come to work for many years for the Corporation.

Josh James Gillies, great grandson of Arthur Temple, with you-know-who.

Jimmy Jnr's, wife Rose née Barber also worked as a conductress in the 1940s. Jimmy Snr was to endure a long-term illness, which he was to bear with his usual dignity, before succumbing to it in May 1960.

Jimmy would have been proud to know that his great-grandson, Arthur's grandson, Joshua James Gillies, aged 10, would be following in his footballing footsteps, as Josh has just signed schoolboy forms for Newcastle United.

Arthur Temple, storekeeper.

Jimmy Temple Snr, ex-Sunderland footballer.

On the 3rd August 1934 an experimental bus operation began, a circle route, along the sea front to Whitburn and back to Seaburn. The service was unique in that it was to use a new type of bus called 'the tram-o-car', also known as the 'Toast Rack' because of its appearance. The bus was painted in a bright red colour and was operated by only a driver. Was this the beginning of 'one-man buses'? One of the first drivers to take this vehicle on service was George Richmond, a small jolly man as I remember him, an ideal personality for this kind of summer operation. In 1939 these buses were to be 'covered in' by panelling in the sides. The initiative being that of Charlie Hopkins, the buses were given another nickname, that of 'Charlie's Taxis'.

The tram-o-car used in summer time on a Whitburn Circular around 1934.

Barbara Morrison, my aunt, was born 11th May 1905 in Hendon, Sunderland. She was a lady with a rough exterior but a very soft centre, borne out by her affection for her sisters and brothers, especially her youngest brother, my father. Aunt Babs, as we all knew her, was to be like a mother to him, washing and ironing his clothes, making his meals and being his general dog's body right up to him getting married, aged 27. Babs would never marry, but I do believe that there was someone in her life, although I never found out for definite. Along with one of her sisters, Annie, Babs became a wartime conductress, but unlike Annie who left when the war ended, she continued to work on. During which time she met Celia Seth,

Celia Seth (left) and Babs Morrison (my aunt), circa 1940.

another conductress, with whom a great, and, lifelong friendship would develop. Celia began working on the buses as a war conductress, and began taking care of Babs almost from the first day. My aunt was diabetic, and would slowly, but surely, fail in her health, and eventually, she was to go blind. Celia was there all the time, even though, towards the end of Babs' life, her own health was failing. Barbara passed away 22nd March 1998, and less than three years later, Celia was to succumb on 1st January 2001. Friends and companions all the way.

Another very good friend to both Babs and Celia, and someone who I am grateful to for supplying me with information, was Bob Taylor. Being just a young man of 70 now, Babs and Celia thought of him as their son, and cared for him accordingly. I am sure that Bob will miss them both very much. Many thoughts and memories.

Violet Buddle and Vera Garrick, also great friends for many years, even after they both finished work as conductresses. Both Vi and Vera socialised together, along with their husbands. Vera's husband Fred also worked for many years as a driver for the Corporation, and on 18th December 1964 he received a 30 years long service award. Vi continued to work as a conductress, and then, when the new token system began in 1966, she began working in the shop selling tokens, where she retired. Not satisfied with working all those years on the trams and buses, Vi still continues to work, and at the time of writing, she is in her 80s. God bless ya chuck.

Conductresses Violet Buddle (left) and Vera Garrick.

Brenda Johnson
Conductress
1950s-1986

Betty Charlton
Conductress
1951-1986

Martha Naisbett
Conductress
1954-1978

Emily Meadows
Conductress
1950s-1970s

Doris Trotter
Conductress
1950s-1970s

Sylvia Barnes
Conductress
1956-1986

Eleanor Brannigan
Conductress
1950s-1986

Edith Brownl
Conductress
1950s-1986

Pat Slater
Conductress
1959-1986

Betty Derivan
Conductress
1950s-1986

A young slip of a girl began a 41 years service as a temporary ticket clerk in 1932. Miss Annie Lancaster was to work her way up to become the general manager's secretary after becoming a short hand typist. She had many other tasks to perform, including the organising of the Seaburn Illuminations, which were a very popular attraction in the 1930s and '40s. The staff, during the Second World War, were to organise a Home Guard of their own and Miss Lancaster volunteered her services as telephonist and secretary. Annie took her well deserved retirement in 1973 and she was looking forward to visiting the European countries that she had not already visited.

As in the First World War woman were to, once again, play a major part in the workings of the Corporation Transport Department. Women were recruited almost before the war

Annie Lancaster, manager's secretary 1932-1973.

Wartime drivers and conductresses with Inspector Muriel Newton in centre with skirt on.

started. With the Company having learnt from their experiences during the First War, there were many differences in how the women were treated.

Although still not equal to their male colleagues, wages wise, conductresses were receiving £3 10s in 1943, while a young man could take home £4 10s 0d. Conditions were much improved better uniforms, better training, canteens and better social conditions.

Even so, with war raging, and coming yet closer to home with the bombing, the woman were under enormous strain to carry on in such conditions. Many of them were mothers and although grandma was probably the babysitter, I'm sure the children were still uppermost in the minds of mother while carrying out her duty.

Wartime conductresses, rear, left to right: Helen Binns, Annie Lennox, Dolly Atkinson. Front: Lyala Anderson, Emma Carr and Molly Parker.

Many characters were to emerge during the following years, people like 'Gonger' Dobson. We don't know who is responsible for the 'gong', but we do know that the constant misuse of it gave 'Gonger' his name for the rest of his life. What is a gong? Well it is an instrument that was designed to give warning to pedestrians that a tram was approaching. The gong was an old engine valve, which was rapped in a piece of sponge from an old tram seat. It was then inserted in a hole in the tram floor so when the driver pressed the valve down the bell would ring. When the valve was released the sponge would then expand and then the process was ready again, Go for it 'Gonger!!!!'

H.W. Snowball, manager 1948-1952.

After Charlie Hopkins, Mr Henry W. Snowball, who had been with the Corporation since 1926 as rolling stock manager, was appointed General Manager. He had been assistant manager since 1945, and after his appointment in 1948 he was to serve only three more years as General Manager until his death in 1952.

Mr Norman Morton succeeded Charlie Hopkins as the next manager of Sunderland Corporation Transport and was to become the manager, by no fault of his own, to see the end of the trams and the complete takeover of buses. Mr Morton tried to improve where Mr Hopkins left off, but through interference of many factors, he was unable to fight against the Transport Committee of the time, and so, he eventually give in and resigned in October 1967. Norman Morton, before coming to Sunderland, had served with the R.E.M.E. where he commanded workshops in India. Manchester-born he was also director of the Road Haulage Executive for Northampton and Nottingham. Both Manchester and Southport Corporation employed him

Mr Norman Morton, manager 1954-1967.

where he learnt his trade in transport. After leaving Sunderland he took up the post of research officer in traffic engineering for the Department of Civil Engineering. In March 1972, while visiting a friend, Mr Norman Morton passed away. He was still employed by the Civil Engineering Department, and was about to leave for advisory work in Malaysia, when his death occurred. His wife, his son and two daughters survived Norman. His memory will live on in Sunderland for as long as the public travel on the one-man buses, for which Norman was solely responsible. Thank you Norman Morton.

The trams of Sunderland were to take their final bow on 1st October 1954. On that day, or should we say, night, the trams were to disappear in great pomp and circumstance. Including 86 tram, the last official tram, there were 8 other trams carrying out various tasks to enable members of the Transport Committee, and members of the public to take part in the procession. The other trams taking part were No. 34, which carried members of the public and was destroyed on 15th November 1954, along with No. 31 tram which also carried the public. Trams Nos. 24, 32, and 93 which all carried the public, in

Derek Allsop
Driver
1972-Today

Kevin Bell
Driver/Instructor
1972-Today

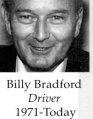

Billy Bradford
Driver
1971-Today

Les Stratton
Driver
1971-2000

John Callaghan
Conductor/Driver
1964-1997

Arthur Burgess
Driver
1968-Today

Gil Shotton
Conductor/Driver
1959-1996

Freddy Gibbons
Driver
1967-Today

Billy Southern
Driver
1955-1986

Billy Connolly
Driver
1950s-1970s

Tram No. 34 (2) carried members of the public.

Tram No. 31 (2) carried members of the public.

Tram No. 35 (2) carried members of the public.

Tram No. 24 (2) carried members of the public.

Tram No. 32 (2) carried members of the public.

Tram No. 91 carried the Transport Band.

Tram No. 96 carried the guests of Corporation.

Tram No. 93 carried members of the public.

Tram No. 86 the official last tram to run in Sunderland getting ready for its final journey outside Wheatsheaf Depot 1st October 1954. Kneeling at the side of the tram is Tommy Holmes.

Rear, left to right: Con J.J. Glendenning and Chief Inspector John (Jack) Thomas Roberts. Front: Ald. R.T. Weston, Ald. Mrs H.E. Blacklock (Mayor) unknown, unknown, unknown, Clr. Atkinson, Mr N. Morton manager S.C.T and Clr Wilkinson.

Lifting the tramlines near the Sun Inn at Southwick, circa 1955.

January 1954 the burning of Tram Nos. 48, 49 and 53 on the Block Yard, Roker.

October, were to meet the same fate as the previous trams, and were to 'meet their maker' at the same time in November '54.

No. 91 tram was to take it's place in history by carrying the Transport Band, to ensure a rousing but musical farewell, but it too was to go to the scrapyard in November.

No. 96 tram was to meet the same fate, after carrying the guests of the Corporation on that night, as all the other trams and go the 'yard'. As mentioned earlier 86 tram was the official 'Last Tram to run in Sunderland' and carried the official party including the Mayor. It was not given any preferential treatment because of its place it would take in history, and so it too went to be dismantled on 15th November 1954.

It must be remembered that a total of 9 trams ended the history of trams in Sunderland, and we must also take into account that there were 9 last drivers and possibly 9 last conductors, who were to play their part.

So when people say 'my father, or, my grandfather, was on the last tram', they could be right.

Henry Milley
Conductor
1967-1976

Norman Kirkbride
Conductor
1969-1973

Bobby Barnes
Conductor/Cashier
1960s-1980s

Fred Cooperwaite
Conductor/Cashier
1965-1986

Jimmy Day
Conductor
1961-1964

Cec Griffiths
Conductor
1950s-1986

Bobby Money
Conductor/Cashier
1950s-1980s

Joe Boddam
Driver
1950s-1986

Gordon Kirkpatrick
Driver
1950s-1980s

Harry Hughes
Conductor
1940s-1986

When I began researching this book one of the first names I was to come across was that of Ernie Quin. I had worked for 27 years with the Corporation, and yet, I had never even heard his name. I cannot understand why, because from the information I have collected he must have been a real busy person on behalf of the staff, certainly the kind of man I could have admired, and respected, and maybe have got on well with.

Ernie Quin (driver).

Ernie was involved in all kinds of things which involved the staff. He was secretary for the Institute, involving arranging all kinds of social events, his favourite was the children's field day, outings for the retired members, dinners, and Christmas celebrations, and one of the fairly new functions, the Safety Awards for drivers and more recently, conductors. It was regarding these awards that I came in touch with the activities of

Mary Quin (conductress/cleaner), 1960.

Tower Wagon with the driver Joe Quin.

Ernie. He should have been organising the function for 1957, when he would have received his own Safety Award of a five year medal, having accumulated the first four years certificates in succession. However, Ernie was not well and was resting in the Royal Infirmary, recovering from a stomach operation. Because of his previous endeavours with his organising for others, Ernie was to have a surprise regarding his award. Mr Norman Morton the General Manager took Ernie's medal into the ward and pinned the medal on his chest.

Ernie Quin began on the Corporation in 1925 as a points boy, he then went in the shed as a shed boy before becoming a conductor. In 1935 he became a tram driver, which he enjoyed most of all, and then with the demise of the trams, he took to bus driving, which I am told, he wasn't very happy with. Ernie's illness took hold and he passed away peacefully at home on 10th November 1958 aged just 50. At first I couldn't find a photograph of Ernie, and I was having difficulty in finding any information about him, until quite by accident I met his son, Brian. Brian Quin had only been working for the Corporation for about 35 years, and I had known him all the time that I had worked there, but I just never connected Brain with Ernie.

As well as father and son, there was also mum, Mary. She was to work for a short time after Ernie's death, as a conductress first, then as a cleaner in the depot. One of the first horse drawn tram drivers, born in 1872 , was none other than Ernie Quin's father, Joseph Quin, Joseph was to start work for the Tramways Company in 1886 as a horse boy, he then had various jobs as, conductor, tram driver, and he then drove the Tower Wagon when the electric trams started running. Joe died whilst still in the employ of the Tramways in 1925, he was 53 years old. The story ends when Joseph's other son, Joseph Jnr, was to become a conductor, making the family complete. Joe Jnr only stayed for a short while having been involved in an accident. He passed away in 1961, three years after his brother Ernie. The good news is that Brian Quin is still employed by the Corporation's successors, Stagecoach.

Joe Quin Snr, horse drawn tram driver/ over head trolley driver.

Joe Quin Jnr, tram driver 1912-21

Brian Quin, store keeper.

Many of the tram and bus conductors were to become popular personalities with the public, and one such person was Mary Shields née Parker. Cheerful, helpful and considerate 'Molly', as she later became known, also took great pains in ensuring that she would be punctual, as well as pleasantly, turned out for work. She was to be rewarded for her pains when she was awarded

Left to right: Tommy Douglas, driver, Mary 'Molly' Parker, conductress and Charlie Carter, inspector.

the B.E.M. She never missed a shift throughout the whole period of the war – a rare feat in those days. When the trams disappeared from the streets Molly became a bus conductress, and was to be on the first bus in service to pass through Park Lane bus station when it opened in 1958. On the 13th February 1960 an accident occurred involving a cyclist, and Molly being ever helpful, left her bus to give assistance, she herself was hit by a passing car and was badly injured. Molly was taken to the Royal Infirmary, but unfortunately her injuries were so bad she passed away. So well respected was Molly that the public turned out in vast numbers at her funeral to pay their last respects. Both the public and the staff remember even to this day Molly with fond affection.

Although she could have been conscripted to work, Mary Jane Elizabeth Rackstraw, was one of the early volunteers who enrolled with the Corporation during the Second World War. Mary joined in 1942, and was soon enjoying her stint as a conductress, along with another 65 women conductresses who had either volunteered themselves or had been volunteered by the government of the day. In the same year Charlie Hopkins asked Mary if she would like to try her hand at tram driving and she jumped at the chance, along with another two ladies.

By the end of the war there would be a number of lady tram drivers, but Mary, as history would reveal, was the first. After the war she worked in the depot as a cleaner, until she retired in 1954. Mary was to enjoy only a short retirement and passed away in August 1960.

Tram driver Mary Jane Rackstraw around 1942.

Doreen Whitwell joined the Corporation 1977 as secretary to Alan Wright.

Cyril Pace
Driver/Inspector
1940s-1986

David Duncan
Inspector
1970-1998

Nobby Clarke
Driver/Inspector
1958-1986

Jacky Brannigan
Driver/Inspector
1947-1986

Teddy Hownam
Inspector
1940s-1970s

Elijah Evans
Driver/Inspector
1940s-1980s

Alfie Bennett
Driver/Inspector
1950s-1980s

Ronnie Gamblin
Driver/Inspector
1950s-1980s

George Whitfield
Driver/Inspector
1950s-1980s

Sammy Rodgers
Driver/Inspector
1972-1994

When I had been with the Corporation for about a year, in 1970, one of the best conductors I had the pleasure of working with, and one of the characters, was Harry Hodgson. Harry was well known by the passengers, for his wit and ways. He would entertain the public by, sometimes cracking a joke, or shouting out the stop coming up, in his own way. 'Royal in for Mary', for the Royal Infirmary, he'd shout, 'Gan inside and put sum coal on tha fire' in the winter, 'last one downstairs, put the leets out' was another cry from Harry, when the bus was on its last journey. Harry charmed everyone with his stories, but the best stories he kept for our tea breaks, either at the terminus or in the canteens. Not many of the public were aware of Harry's past, but if you were to look closely at his gait, the way he walked, or should I say, the way he shuffled along, you could maybe see just a little of his past.

Harry 'Ginger Wilson' Hodgson, conductor.

Harry Hodgson was an amateur boxer and proud of it. It is not difficult to understand why Harry should have taken to boxing the way he did, his father was none other than Lister Hodgson, a bare knuckle fighter of the early 1900s. Lister fought in the booths at many fairgrounds, and he earned many a coin fighting a bear from Professor Moore's fair, and sometimes he won. Harry took the name of 'Ginger Wilson' to carry out his boxing exploits. He was small in height, but certainly big in heart and bravery, because of his stature, most of his opponents were much taller, such a man was Toby Carr. Carr was a full six inches taller than Ginger, and by his appearance, much stronger. According to Harry, his fears were borne out in the first round, when Carr had him down for a count of 8, and in the second round when Harry went down again, this time for a count of 9. In the third round, which proved to be the last, Harry had noticed that Carr was jumping each time he suffered a body blow, so, Harry summoned up all his strength and hit Carr with a blow to the solar plexus. His opponent jumped in pain and hit the floor unable to continue. There is a twist to this story of course. The official referee had not turned up, and a certain Lister Hodgson would referee the fight. Of course there was nothing untoward went on, you cannot fiddle a knockout, not even for your own son. Can you?

Harry would leave his beloved boxing after suffering some damage to his liver after a fight with Ryhope's Billy Lawrence. 'He was the only man to really hurt me. He could really hit hard for round after round and never get tired of it' recalled Harry.

Henry William Bolam Hodgson aka Ginger Wilson, also took his place in the Second World War, and after his return, he gave up his job as a furniture machinist to come and work for the Corporation as a driver first of all, and then after an accident, he became a conductor. Harry retired in 1985 and spent a short time with his wife Sarah Ann. When Sarah Ann died, Harry went to live with one of his twin daughters in Stoke. I never saw Harry again, but I heard that he too had passed away in the early '90s. He will be remembered.

James Anderson, horse keeper 1879-1919.

One of the first photographs in the book, showing the horse drawn tram from Roker to Monkwearmouth, is also showing, at the front, holding the horse, Mr James Anderson, horse keeper for Tramways. Information given to me by Trevor Tennant, Mr Anderson's great-grandson, and borne out by records, is that James Anderson before becoming horse keeper, was one of the cabmen in the Fawcett Street incident. Born in 1856, James was 23 when he went to work for the Tramways, and not much more is known about him, other than he was to marry twice, and here he is with his second wife Alice Teasdale, whom he married in 1933, aged 77. It was to be a short marriage, as James passed away in 1939, making Alice a widow for the fourth time.

Tools essential for a tram driver's working day – tea can, watch and gonger.

The person who was to become part of the history of the Sunderland Corporation Transport Department, arrived as Deputy Manager on 13th October 1965. Mr Alan H. Wright took up his appointment, succeeding Mr W.K. Haigh, who became manager of Hull Transport. Mr Wright, an engineer with many qualifications in that field, was assistant motor bus engineer of Manchester City Transport Department, having graduated BSc, from Manchester University. He served a post graduate apprenticeship, from 1951 to '56, with Leyland Motors, and was assistant technical advisor in the research and development department. After two short years, on 9th April 1967, Mr Wright was to become general manager, taking over from Mr R.E. Bottrill, who was taking up the manager's post at Portsmouth Transport. I was lucky to work for Mr Wright, and like the majority of the staff, respected him, so much so, and many years later, he asked me to call him Alan, and I couldn't out of the respect I have for him. As I write about him, I will always refer to him as Mr Wright. Although the development of the traffic and engineering sections of the Transport Department was important, and many changes would take place under Mr Wright, the welfare and social side of the Department would progress and would benefit all of the staff. No longer would the staff be out on their own trying to arrange and develop, but the management would now take an active part. Mr Wrght's idea would be to create an overall governing body and bring all of the various social sections under one umbrella. Along with men such as Austin Robson, Tommy Derivan, Stan Laverick and many others of the day, too

Mr Alan Wright last Manager of Sunderland Corporation Transport.

Skip O'Brien
Tram Driver
1930s-1960s

Billy Hardy
Driver
1950s-1970s

numerous to mention, this idea would eventually succeed, and still continues today, 2001.

Under Mr Wright many changes both in the engineering, and in the traffic side, would take place. The transfer from the set right, to the Ultimate ticket machines, bringing about the Imprest system for conductors and one-man drivers. A central bus station would open near Crowtree Road on 11th December 1967, later, on the 23rd November 1969, the bus station would be fully operational and would provide canteen facilities for the staff. A Zonal fare system would be introduced, incorporating a flat fare of 4d, or one token per zone, later removed when the tokens were to disappear. The one-man operation would be extended, using new single deck Leyland Marshall buses. A new office block replaced the old Wheatsheaf Offices in 1967,

Tommy Smith
Driver
1960s-1980s

Jos Calvert
Driver
1970s-1980s

Les Watt
Conductor/Driver
1963-1996

Eddie Allsop
Tram/Bus Driver
1952-1986

Harry Freeman, manager 1973-1978.

once again improving the conditions of the traffic staff. As was mentioned earlier, the change that Mr Wright will be remembered for, even after all the other good things for which he was responsible, came on the 31st March 1973. That day was to see the end of almost 100 years of Corporation Transport in Sunderland, and was to

'Charlie' Parnaby
Tram/Bus Driver
1937-1977

Tommy Seymour
Driver
1940s

Wheatsheaf Offices today.

Wyn Thomas
Driver
1959-1966

Jacky Fergerson
Driver
1960s-1980s

take Mr Wright into history as the last manager of Sunderland Corporation Transport. On 1st April 1973 the Metropolitan area of Tyneside was to take over all the Public Transport in South Shields and Sunderland and become known as the Passenger Transport Executive. Mr Wright was to become Associate Director and Divisional Manager South, a position he would hold until he retired on 26th October 1986. I believe that, today Mr Wright lives in the Newcastle area, and hopefully is enjoying the happy retirement that he richly deserves. Mr Harry Freeman was to work with Mr Wright as Manager of Sunderland for a short time in 1974. Harry began his time with the Corporation around 1946 as a driver. And worked his way through the ranks to become manager. Definitely strict but fair, he was looked upon as a people's manager, and he too liked nothing better than socialising with his staff. He keenly supported the welfare section of the job, and especially the football team. Harry Freeman retired on 31st August 1978, and passed away 16 years later, 14th May 1994. He did however ensure that in those 16 years he would attend every retired members' outing, so that he was able to continue socialising with his staff.

Influential in many of the changes that were to take place in the early 1960s and '70s was a local boy makes good, Robert Wilkinson 1894-1971. Although the Corporation never employed him, he did have a soft spot for its continued success, and in his various political roles, he was to ensure its progress. Robert was to begin his working life at the age of 14, as a trapper boy down the pit at Wearmouth Colliery. It was during his 50 years as a miner that his political interests were to take hold and he was to serve on the local council for 22 years. Prior to his council work Robert served on the Public Assistance Committee, he was a Governor of the Royal Infirmary, and a member of the Workforce Education Association. He was elected as a councillor in 1945, and Alderman in 1959. After only four years he became Deputy Mayor, and the following year Mayor, 1964-65. As Transport Committee member he attended the end of the trams in 1954, he was to become Chairman of the Committee in 1960. In 1967 Robert Wilkinson retired from the council due to domestic trauma, his wife having passed away a year earlier. Whilst on holiday in Blackpool in 1971 he too sadly passed away aged 77, he was survived by his two sons, Robert and William, 10 grandchildren and a great grandson. One of his granddaughters, Mrs June Mallaburn, still continues the family's association with the Transport. She is employed as a cleaner for Stagecoach, the successors of the Corporation. June's husband David Mallaburn is also an employee, as a fitter, so Robert Wilkinson is still ensuring the continued progress of public transport in Sunderland.

Mayor Alderman Robert Wilkinson.

Transport Committee 1959-1960. Back, left to right: Clr J. Gibson, Ald. W. Harvey, Mrs K. Cohen, Clrs H. Graham, E. Joice and Mr D. Snow (Solicitor). Centre row: Clrs N. Waters, R.W. Shotton, T.W. Hudson, T.M. Carr, C.H. Slater. Ald H.G. Jones, R.T. Weston, Clrs R.B. Spain, J.W.D. Bell. Front: Clr J. Harding, Ald E.E. Wales, Clr J. Little, Ald R. Wilkinson (vice Chairman) Clr T.W. Atkinson (Chairman) Ald N.L. Allison (Mayor) Mr N. Morton (Manager S.C.T.), Clr J.A. Smith and W.D. Stephenson.

On 5th September 1966 the Corporation introduced a triple surprise for the travelling public. A new flat fare system, a new token system and a specially designed vehicle to be able to cope with the new system. Mr Norman Morton had been advocating a flat fare system for some time and here at last, with a few teething troubles, it was about to begin. The introduction of a 4d fare for any journey was something that the public could well do with, and coupled with the token system of 10 tokens for 2/9d, well surely that would be better still, and along with a new single deck bus which had a machine that would accept the new tokens well – UTOPIA. WRONG. The public was about to find that it would possibly cost them more with the new system than with the present. If a passenger were to use a token on a journey that would take them across the town, then because of the Town Centre boundary the passenger would be required to use another token, where as a fare paying passenger who initially paid the 4d could remain on their way without further cost. Surprise to the public in some ways, but the system was announced with much publicity, and, there were many outlets where the new tokens could be bought, including Joplings Stores. The tokens could also be bought from the driver, but on that Monday morning,

Selling bus tokens in Joplings Store, 1966.

Leyland Panther No. 53 bus purpose built for accepting tokens.

Driver Norman Burlison selling tokens on 53 Bus 1966.

passengers had forgot to buy their tokens, and so they were surprised that, although they had already waited in a queue, they were queuing again to pay cash. Let me explain. The new bus had two doors that could be entered, one door on the left for the passenger who wanted to pay cash and needed change, and the other door, on the right, was for passengers with tokens. Because the token passengers needed no change, and just had to put one token in a machine, they bordered much quicker, and so no queues. Which in retrospect was the idea of the token system in the first place. There were many hidden benefits for the staff, not only did the tokens create a new bonus to the wage packets but it also created some new jobs. Staff were needed to empty the token machines when they were full, or when the buses returned to the depots at night. Jimmy

Micky Stanbridge
Driver
1969-Today

Alfie Johnson
Driver
1950s-1970s

Freddie Garrick
Driver
1940s-1970s

Bobby Wheldon
Driver
1940s-1970s

Arthur Priest
Driver
1940s-1986

Colin Stevenson
Driver
1950s-1970s

Harry Poole
Driver
1950s-1970s

Ronnie Shereton
Conductor/Driver
1947-1983

Lofty Johnson
Driver
1950s-1986

Arthur Snowdon
Driver
1950s-1986

George Pescod selling tokens.

Shaw, Union steward, was suffering with his health and so emptying the machines became an ideal job for him. Sadly Jimmy passed away on 4th September 1980.

Jimmy Shaw and May Shaw née O'Brien.

There were also a number of staff required to sell the tokens. People like Vi Buddle, Jacky Hedley, Sylvia Barnes, George Pescod and all the other drivers and conductors. The flat fare and the tokens did prove to be popular in one particular way, and that was with parents that sent their children to school by bus. The children only needed two tokens per day, and therefore it was not necessary for the children to carry any cash, and so it deterred bullies from picking on small children. There was a change in the system 18 months after it was introduced, mainly because of complaints from the public about various cost anomalies, but company costs had changed also. On 5th February 1968 adult fares would be increased to 6d per journey, children journeys 2d and concessionary pass-holders 3d any journey. Tokens were increased to 8 for 3/-. One year later on 6th January 1969 the Zonal System was introduced, dividing the Town into 3 Zones, the fares were to be one token per Zone, 4d cash per zone, and other fares to follow suit, i.e. children and pensioners. Even after decimalization, the token system and flat fare system carried on, unfortunately not long after April 1974, at the end of the Corporation, on 7th October 1974, the tokens, and the flat fare system was withdrawn. Although many other types of machine ticketing were tried, in my opinion the token system was the best, because of its simplicity in operation

The 15th February 1967 was the day that two conductress were to enter the history books. Pat Entwhistle and Joyce Beumont were to take out on service a double deck bus and become the first women bus drivers to do so. Four weeks previous Pat and Joyce were asked to join a Transport Department programme to train women to drive, because of the shortage of drivers in general. They were to train under driving instructor Gerry Dawson, who commented that there was no reason why women shouldn't be able to manage to drive double decks, it would be just a matter of training, and gaining confidence over the size and length of the vehicle. After the month of intensive training, the Ministry of Transport Commissioner tested the women, and they both passed first time. This enabled another two ladies, who were waiting in the wings, to try their hand at driving. Pat Entwhistle was the first, to take out her bus on the

Pat Entwhistle one of the first of two lady double deck bus drivers along with Joyce Beumont.

Grindon route, and Joyce was to take her bus out later in the day. Pat started with the Corporation in 1954 just as the trams were leaving the streets, even then she was dreaming of becoming a bus driver, so why the long wait of thirteen years? 'Well we weren't asked, but when we were, I jumped at the chance' recalled Pat. Although Pat was to remain as a driver, and she was pleased that she would never have to run up and down those stairs, she was willing to take her turn in conducting if she was required to do so. One of Pat's friends Nan Nash was a conductor, and I think they were both pleased that the opportunity came along when they could become a crew and work together all day and every day. After they both retired they moved to Scarborough where they lived until Nan became ill and returned home to Sunderland to stay with her sister Peggy, and in 1987 Nan passed away. Pat remained in Scarborough, where she still lives to this day.

During the many years of the Tramways, and the Corporation, there was to be an abundance of people who were to represent the staff in one way or another. Caring managers, friendly foremen, social minded people, and when history provided them, Union representatives. Men and women who took up the challenge as officers or stewards of their Union branches

Conductress Nan Nash, October 1956.

could, and many of them would, become disillusioned with the job due to the stress of attempting to carry out their normal jobs, and the task of representing their branch members as well. Many names of people involved spring to mind, Ernie Quin, Dickie Bolton, Billy Winter, Austin Robson, Tommy Derivan, Roy Richardson, Bobby Coates, Teddy Laverick, Jimmy Shaw, Edith Brown and Norman Burlison, all Union men and many, many others, good stewards like, Doug Watson, George Taylor, Stan Hepple, and later Micky Stanbridge, Billy Bradford, and lots more, too numerous to mention but not out of mind.

On 5th February 1968, a man was to begin his employment with the Corporation that would have a significant effect on the members of No. Ten Branch, General and Municipal Workers Union. This was the branch that was responsible for the welfare of the drivers and conductors, and some of the engineering staff, of the Corporation Transport in Sunderland. Although it was to be in the era of the P.T.E. the successors of the Corporation when he was to take over, he did do his 'training' in the early '70s. Billy Tarvit became branch Secretary in 1977, and along with Colin Mather, he began surrounding himself with a good committee of stewards. People who would take on extra responsibilities by forming themselves into sub-committees, schedule stewards, engineering stewards, health and safety stewards, and a welfare officer. He ensured that all shop stewards would have the best and correct training by sending them on the relevant educational courses that the Union could provide. This would leave Bill, Colin, and a newcomer, Bob Clay, to get on with the serious business of negotiating with the management for better pay and conditions, and, in the early years they had much success with this formula. Not to detract from the many successes of the men who were mentioned earlier, but because I was there, and was a beneficiary as a driver, Billy, Colin and Bob did improve on all conditions, pay rises were significant, conditions generally improved, better running times, better buses and more holidays. The good times appeared to have arrived, and would continue until 1986. Billy Tarvit as a character was a innovator, a man that could spot and take advantage out of nothing. One such idea was to change the way of ticketing, firstly in Sunderland, and then nationwide, and eventually, worldwide. A different type of ticketing system was being used in almost every town and city in the United Kingdom, Ultimate machines in one town, Almex machines in another city, all with their own way of accounting and collecting systems. It was on a cultural exchange trip to

Arthur Chisholm, clothing store inspector.

Union Secretary Billy Tarvit, conductor/driver.

DBR 649 Daimler Roe body one of the first pre-select gear change vehicles.

Lol Watt
Driver
1959-1993

Tommy Cook
Coach Builder
1950s

Chris Storey
Painter
1950s

George Strong
Driver/Depot
1964-Today

Bob Swallwell
Foreman Engineer
1960s

Ronnie Christie
Depot
1970s

Arthur Lusby
Driver
1960s

Bernie Thompson
Tram Driver/Depot
1948-1986

Stan Copeland
Depot
1950s-1970s

Brian Blyth
Engineer
1960s-1990s

Blackburn Transport where an old manager of Sunderland, Ian Hann, was manager, that Billy Tarvit was to pick up on his claim to fame. Ian Hann had been toying with the idea of converting a mechanical Almex ticket machine into an electrical machine, and he had acquired a number of pamphlets on such ideas, but had never been able to make the conversion, but he did arouse the interest of Billy. Picking up a couple of pamphlets from Ian, Billy was already on to a way of using electronics for ticketing, when we were on the bus coming home from Blackburn. In 1980 a team was set up to explore Billy's ideas, and after involving Almex Ticketing Systems, along with Jeremy Meal, of the P.T.E., the system of using electronically operated ticket machines evolved. Many advantages were to be gained by this kind of ticketing. For the companies, with the use of computers, easy analysis of information. For the staff, no more heavy ticket machine boxes to carry about, but most of all, ticketing systems were able to become universal, and would be quite able, and easy to evolve. Many other kinds of tickets could be sold on buses, such as travel tickets, weekly, or monthly, and even yearly. The staff expressed some concerns about spies in the cab but the majority of the staff could see the advantages of the new system and soon got to grips with it.

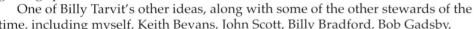

Colin Mather, conductor/driver/ Union Chairman 1969-1987.

One of Billy Tarvit's other ideas, along with some of the other stewards of the time, including myself, Keith Bevans, John Scott, Billy Bradford, Bob Gadsby, George Kenny, Micky Stanbridge, and Clive Fallon, was to set up and investigate the new Credit Union loans and savings system which had just came out of America. After a number of months of investigation, along with the Joint Negotiation Committee, the Busways Credit Union was set up in 1989, and today it is one of the most successful in the British Isles. Billy was to be elected as Secretary of the Credit Union from the beginning, and after leaving his job with Busways in 1996 he was given the post of full time manager of the Credit Union and he still holds the post today. One of Billy's proudest moments came on 1st March 1991 when he received a Certificate of Merit, a token of appreciation for services to the Trade Union Movement in the Northern Region. The Certificate takes pride of place behind Billy's desk in the Credit Union Office in Waterloo Place.

J. Colin Mather was to become a very good friend of mine and, luckily for many other future staff that Colin was to represent, there good friend too. As the Union Chairman, Colin cared for the members totally without any discrimination and saved many men's job when they were up for discipline. Colin's other contribution was to add to the English dictionary by coining the word 'T'w'erly'. The full meaning of the word stems from the senior citizens of Sunderland cry at nine-thirty in the morning, 'Am I too early for my pass?' Colin began to use the phrase as an expression of endearment such as, 'they should let the t'w'erlies ride all day!'

Trevor Tennant, began working for the Corporation in 1968, but picked up his nickname in 1982. Tipper or Turnover Tennant as he has been known as since bonfire night of that year, was involved in a regrettable accident. As usual the weather was atrocious, heavy rain had been falling for most of the day, and was continuing to fall when the accident occurred. Due to the slippery road conditions at the junction of Silksworth Lane and Christopher Road at the Barnes in Sunderland, the double deck bus driven by Trevor, skidded and toppled over on to the top of a passing car. The combined injured, numbered thirteen people, including a two month old baby, Lee Sumby. Speaking to Trevor after the accident, he said that the bus just started to tip over very slowly, and just lent on to the car, rather than falling on to it. History repeating itself with the comparison with Tram No. 70 in Hylton Road, 15th June 1933. It too fell to the ground slowly, being supported by the overhead cables. After the accident, and after the seriousness of it died down, Trevor began to take a little ribbing from the rest of the staff, turn the tele over Trev, have you got any tips for us today Trev, and so it went on for quite some time. Trevor takes it all in his stride, and says that he can take it all, as long as no one was seriously injured in the accident, that was his only worry.

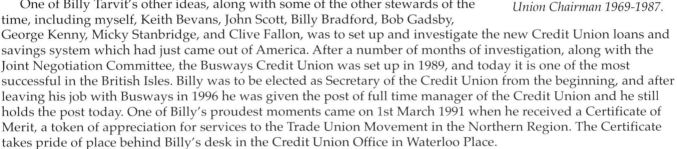

Trevor Tennant

Silksworth Lane, 1st November 1982.

Hylton Road, 15th June 1933.

Two events took place in 1971, one that took me a while to understand and which I didn't enjoy, and the other I was fully aware of, and was over the moon about. On the 15th February 1971 many of the staff and all of the nation would be most confused, not only about travelling, but shopping in general. That day was D-day – the beginning of decimalization. What an impact it had on the fares, and, what an impact it had on everyone, young and elderly alike would suffer. The management of the Corporation had made valiant attempts to educate the public prior by advising them to purchase tokens to help adjust to the difference in the value between £ s d and decimal. Unfortunately the advice went unheeded, and so panic ensued, and took a while to subside. Although children had been educated about the new coinage, it still took a while for them to grasp the change. Just to change a letter from D to P was complicated enough, but to mentally change pennies to pence and carry out the task while concentrating on driving as well was a nightmare. One shilling, worth 12 pennies, became 5 pence. Two shillings, worth 24 pennies, became 10 pence, and so on. It was advised that passengers should try and tender their fares in multiples of sixpences, so that the correct decimal change could be given should the passenger require change. The tokens were a little easier to work with as a packet of ten tokens before D-day, cost 3 shillings, and post D-day they could be bought for 15 pence. Easy to buy and easy to spend on fares. Just for the young here is a table of conversion.

	Old	New
One pound	240 pennies	= 100 pence
Ten shillings	120 pennies	= 50 pence
Five shillings	60 pennies	= 25 pence
Half-crown (two shillings and sixpence)	30 pennies	= $12\frac{1}{2}$ pence
Florin or two shillings	24 pennies	= 10 pence
One shilling	12 pennies	= 5 pence
Sixpence	6 pennies	= $2\frac{1}{2}$ pence

New at 15th February 1971 – 2 pence, 1 pence and $\frac{1}{2}$ pence

Later the half pence coin would be taken out of circulation and the cost of items would be rounded UP to the nearest pence. I am certain that even today, 30 years after D-day, that the elderly citizens of our community still count their cash in £ s d, I know I still do at times.

Alan Barnes
Duty Officer
1960-1992

Ken Duncan
Personnel Officer
1950s-1980s

Bob Smith
Chief Cashier
1940s-1970s

Tom Bainbridge
Payroll Officer
1940s-1970s

Harry Tindle
Cashier
1950s-1970s

Jean Culleton
Records
1948-1982

Walter 'Jock' Mann
Conductor/Cashier
1950s-1986

Freddie Young
Duty Officer
1940s-1970s

Learning to exchange £ s d for decimal coins 15th February 1971. Left to right: Austin Robson, Gerry Dawson, Bobby Coates, Alan Barnes, Harry Wallace, Nicky Carter and Norman Burlison.

Gerry Dawson
Driving Instructor
1930s-1970s

Harry Hickman
Inspector
1950s-1970s

The second event of 1971, of which I was part, was to become a piece of sporting history in the transport world. For the third and final time Sunderland Corporation would reach the final of the national trophy, the Cadwallder Cup. Having played in the earlier rounds, I was 'rested' for the semi-final at Hull. However, I still gave my total support to the team for the rest of the competition. George Duncan the manager of the side, and the ever present and enthusiastic Jack Hedley, guided the team with great success in that year, Gerry Fannon and Les Watt made sure that the team was at the peak of physical condition. The day of the semi-final began with a touch of sadness, when Mr Wright announced that his assistant manager Mr Joe Scott had passed away that morning. Mr Scott would have attended the match as usual, as he was an avid supporter of any of the transport teams. The trip to Hull Transport for the game was uneventful and the match it self was not a great one. But we did win 1-0, and we were through to the Final against the southern final winners, Aldershot Traction. The journey home took a turn for the worse. We had used a double deck bus for the trip, and on the way back, somewhere between Hull and York, along a country road, a wagon discharged a large chock of wood from its trailer. The wood went straight through the windscreen narrowly missing the driver, Gerry Fannon. We had to push out the whole of the windscreen for the safety of the passengers who were downstairs, and so that we were able to drive home. The weather was dismal, sleet and snow, it was cold as well, but with all the drivers on the bus taking a 20 minute spell at the wheel we managed to get home. The biggest shock came when the organisers of the bus were given a warning from Mr Wright about how they had put the safety of the rest of the passengers at risk. However everyone on the bus rallied together in support and explained the situation to Mr Wright, that we would have been in more danger if we had stopped

Speedman Robson, 'Speedy' as he was known by workmates and the travelling pubic alike, came to the Wheatsheaf in 1956. He came to the Transport Corporation after a long and charismatic career in the Merchant Navy, giving boxing exhibitions for such celebrities such as, Charlie Chaplin, Primo Carnera and many others. He served on some of the great liners: *Mauritania*, *Queen of Bermuda*, *Homeric* and the *Olympia*. Speedy's quality of entertainment didn't end in the navy as many readers will recall. Speedy was the conductor who would give the call 'gan 't the front pet the fires on' or 'gan up stairs 't the gas chamber' or 'put the lights out when ya cum downstairs'. He had many little jokes that he would share with the passengers and I am sure that he kept them all entertained on many a cold morning. It was a very sad day in August 1970 when after a sort illness 'Speedy' passed away, he was a miss at the time and he will be continued to missed by all.

where we were. Because of the adverse weather conditions we could have frozen and so everyone had agreed that we should make our way home, and so everyone was responsible for the actions that were taken, and responsible for their own safety. The incident was forgotten about.

The Final against Aldershot Traction was at Roker Park, home of Sunderland AFC. It is the dream of every local supporter who plays amateur football to play on their hometown ground and this team was no different. Every one of the team gave that little bit extra in the league games that we played to try and get their place in the final team for the Final. But George and Jacky could only pick 12 players, and to their good judgement, they picked the best team. We were to win convincingly 4-0, centre forward Tommy Agnew,

The 1971 Cadwallder Cup-winning side. Back, left to right: George Duncan (driver) manager, George Peverley (driver), Kevin Taylor (engineer), George McDermid (driver), Jimmy Smurthwaite (driver), Davy Polley (driver), Harry Makka (driver), Lyndon Davison (driver), Gerry Fannon (conductor) trainer. Front: Les Watt (conductor) trainer, Arthur Peverley (driver), Terry McBay (driver), Tommy Surtees (driver), Tommy Agnew (driver), George Flynn (driver) and standing Jacky Hedley (conductor) secretary.

picked up two goals, but should have got more. George McDermid, ex-Sunderland player, played in midfield, and scored a cracker of a goal in the second half. Terry McBay, the other midfielder, also scored. Jimmy Smurthwaite, goalkeeper did not have much to do but played to his usual high standard. He was well covered by the two Peverley brothers, Arthur and Jacky. Kevin Taylor and George Flynn easily controlled the game with their reading of the game and both were instrumental in assisting with the goals. On the left wing was Harry Makka, one of the fastest talents and crosser of a ball I had seen in amateur football. He was well assisted by Davy Polley who fed Harry with many pin-pointed passes. Tommy Surtees, who was the Billy Bremner of the team, hard but fair, certainly lived up to his name, ensuring that although the ball may pass him, the player would not. Tommy's normal contribution. Unfortunately Lyndon Davison, the reserve centre half was not used, and I'm sure he must have felt absolutely terrible after not playing on Roker Park, but he showed no emotion either way, and to his credit, he joined in all the celebrations.

The first time that the football team won the national trophy was in 1962 when they played Cardiff City Transport at Roker Park. Entering the competition for the previous seven years, and reaching the semi-final three times, this was the first time they had reached the Final. Team manager Jack Hedley had guided the team to many local successes in the Ryhope and District Wednesday League, but this was his proudest moment to date. Winning 2-0, with Dave Shillito netting the first and Billy Doran getting the winner, both goals coming in the first half. The Cardiff team were typical Welsh sportsmen, hard, physical, but skilful, and it showed in the second half. The Sunderland defence held together well by Roy Richardson, Tommy Reed and Geordie Curle were able to stem the tide, and feed the forwards

All requests for leave of absence on account of bad colds, headaches, sick relatives, funerals, weddings...........must be handed to the Head of Department before 10 a.m. on the morning of the match!

Request for leave of absence form.

Ronnie Francis
Driver
1940s-1970s

Roy Richardson
Conductor/Driver
1955-1986

Tommy Derivan
Driver
1940s-1970s

Bob Taylor
Driver
1940s-1970s

Martin Hindmarsh
Driver
1950s-1970s

Billy Smith
Conductor/Driver
1950s-1970s

Stan Hepple
Driver
1950s-1970s

John Lounds
Tram/Bus Driver
1940s-1970s

Arthur Walker
Driver
1940s-1970s

George Bostock
Driver
1940s-1970s

The 1962 Cadwallder Cup semi-finalists, Back, left to right: Arthur Lloyd (driver) chairman, Jimmy Day (conductor), G. Curle (driver), Roy Richardson (driver) captain, Kenny Bradburn (driver), Norman Burlison (driver), Tony Lyons (driver), Jack Hedley (conductor) secretary. Front: Bobby Douglas (driver), Billy Doran (driver), Dave Shillito (driver), unknown and Wyn 'Taffy' Thomas (driver).

Cairns, Hall and Sunderland's own Welsh wizard, Wyn Thomas. The goalkeeping giant Kenny Bradburn was kept busy all of the game, but kept a clean sheet. With full back Jimmy Day getting down the wings and Bobby Alderson taking a more defensive role, the Sunderland Transport ran out worthy winners.

In February 1967 the team was to reach the national final for the second time. Having disposed of Birkenhead 1-1, 5-3, Grimsby 3-3, 5-1 and then Rotherham 7-1, with Tommy Agnew scoring four goals in each of the three winning games, they had to meet South Shields in the Northern Final. The game was to be played at Roker Park with an evening kick off. With a 3-1

Cadwallder Cup winners at Roker Park, 4th April 1962, players and officials included: Jacky Hedley (manager), Arthur Lloyd (trainer), Roy Richardson (captain), Tommy Reed, George Curle, Billy Doran, Davy Shillito, Jimmy Day, Kenny Bradburn, Bobby Alderson, ? Hall, Norman Burlison, George Cairns and The Mayor Robert Wilkinson.

win the final result, Tommy Agnew adding another two goals to his name, the team then went on to meet Walsall in the Final. This was played at Fellows Park, Walsall. The game once again was an evening kick-off, adding to travelling difficulties for the Sunderland side, but it made little difference to the result. With Tommy Agnew and Maurice Mitchell, getting one a piece in the second half, Sunderland ran out easy winners. Team captain Alan Wilson lifted the trophy for his hard working team of Roy Richardson, Ray Dodds, Tommy Searle, Vic Avery, Jacky Wiason, Tony Gordon, Joe Drennan, and Bobby Armstrong, with the ever present secretary Jacky Hedley. The long journey home would not seem so long. Well done Sunderland.

Not to be out done or overawed by the men, the ladies of the Corporation formed their own team, and in 1970 they took their team on the road. On August Bank Holiday Monday their match against Brain Mills was one of the major items of the day. It was the first match the Transport Teezers played and with the opposition, The Brian Mills Babes, playing their third game, the Teezers were in for a little bit of a shock. The Babes, playing in front of a large crowd, ran out easy winners by a score of 9-0, but the Teezers were not too downhearted. In their first two games, the Babes had won, 13-1 and 10-0, so at least the Teezers had kept the score down to single figures, and they raised

Charity football match against Brian Mills Babes at Newcastle Road Hospital Ground on 25th May 1970. Left to right: Sylvia Barnes (conductress), Taffy Prosser (driver), Ivy Ross, Doreen Hepple, Christine Hepple, unknown (kneeling), Hazel Hardy, Mayor W.O. Stephenson, Babes, Babes, Babes, Mandy Bould, Eleanor Brannigan, Betty Charlton, Babes, Babes, Martha Nesbitt, Norman Burlison, all the rest are from Brian Mills Babes.

A Corporation cricket team at Leeds in 1962. Back row, left to right: Duggie Watson (driver), Tommy Gardner (driver), Gordon Potts, Stan Hepple (driver), Norman Pewell (depot), Jim Coggins. Front: Tommy Wright, Albert Milner, Freddie Young (duty officer), Harry Tutin (conductor) and Thomas Stafford.

quite a sum for charity. Another long established section was the Corporation cricket team. It too was to have much success in the local leagues, but not, unfortunately, in the national competitions. Although they did reach the Northern Final at Sheffield, and had they won instead of losing by one run, they would have played London in the national Final. Stan Hepple was responsible for the team's early success, while Billy Youern would take over in later years. The team played in the Ryhope and District Wednesday League, and although many trophies would come their way, with changes to shift patterns at work, they felt that the successes could have been greater.

Many other sporting sections were either to appear or were already around. The rambling club had been around since 1902 at least and left a reminder (see snippets 1902). Sections like the Tenpin bowling, sprang up in the sixties with the Americanization of England's society, and, Rock and Roll appearing on the scene. Darts were to have a section when the professional darts player appeared. With

Cricket team, Ryhope and District Wednesday League runners-up 1972. Back, left to right: Keith Sunley (driver), Ian Hann (admin), Fred Anderton (admin), Kenny Watkins (driver), Billy Shergold (driver), Dennis Austin (driver), George Garrett (engineer). Front: Johnny Jobling (engineer), Tommy Agnew (driver), Billy Youern Snr (driver) and Billy Youern Jnr.

George Laidler
Engineer
1940s-1970s

Jimmy Flowers
Tram Body Builder
1940s-1970s

Norman Powell
Depot Foreman
1940s-1970s

Alec Whickham
Storeman
1940s-1970s

Clive Fallon
Fitter
1971-Today

Dickie Bolton
Driver
1930s-1960s

Norman Burlison
Driver/Depot
1950s-1970s

Ralph Parnaby
Conductor/Depot
1920s-1960s

Stan 'Taffy' Johnson
Conductor/Depot
1940s-1970s

Harold Blackband
Conductor
1966-1968

In 1902 the Rambling Club took a walk for charity and an anonymous scribe made a record of the event.

A Memento of the Sunderland Corporation Tramways Employees
G R E A T WALK TO WHITE MARE POOL AND BACK. Sunday 26th July 1903

I'll ask your kind attention, which I hope you'll give, bedad,
And I'll tell you of the walking race the Sunderland
Tramways had
There was over 40 entered for this very big event,
Each one paid his tanner, and on winning he was bent.
There were handymen and cleaners there, and motormen as
well
And skinny-legged conductors well, in fact, the truth tell,
There was nothing else but walking men and men who
knew the track.
On the Sunday morn the Tram men walked to White Mare
Pool and back.

Every one of them toed the mark,
Gus Reed shouted go!
Away they went at a terrible speed,
And didn't they puff and blow,
All the folks for miles around were lined along the track
To see the Sunderland Tram men walk
To White Mare Pool and back.

Clem Humphries gave a guinea; he's a champion sort, is
Clem
Cordner gave a ton of coal, and blowed good coal as well
Mr Walter Bellsham gave a twelve and sixpenny prize-
An alarm clock, which I'll guarantee, would make a dead
man rise

David Wolfe, the jeweller, of course we went to see,
He gave a prize worth 10/6 as freely as could be
And Mr R.O. Fletcher deserves a little praise-
He gave a pair of Operas, for the fifth man on the race.

Now days before, the race came off, the betting it was great,
It was even money Theakstone and 3 to 1 on Tate.
Dennis stood at 4 to 1, and Bradford stood at twos,
There was some that couldn't stand at all; they'd mopped up
too much booze.
There was fifteen bob on one lad, his condition it was pink
I've heard it said he trained on eggs and Cleveland Dairy
Milk,
And Tommy Carroll swore that his conductor he would sack
If he didn't win the walking race to White Mare Pool and
back.

Gus Reed was the starter, timekeeper as well,
Ned House paced the winner, and, begum, he did it well.
Tulip drove the four-in-hand to take the judges round
I made a book and laid good odds, they knew that I was
sound,
Dennis came in winner, Bradford came in next.
Nunton came in third man, and his backers they were vexed
Bill robe broke teetotal, and blamed his brother Jack.
When Dennis won the Tram men's race to White Mare Pool
and back.

all of these, and other sports being taken up by the staff, names like Johnny Jobling (tenpin), Joe Chick (darts) and Davy Gowland (rambling), all spring to mind, all with many others. In 1952, on a one-off, a team set out to become famous. At Vaux Sports Ground, on the Corporation's annual sports day, the Tug-of-War team took on Vaux for the first time and won. Led by Gordon Smith, a small but well-built man, the team beat Vaux by two pulls to one, and it is believed, that this was the first time the opposition had been defeated.

Tug-O-War team winners 1957. Back, left to right: Billy Middlewood (conductor), Cyril Pace (conductor/driver/inspector), Eric Liddle (conductor), Billy Southern (conductor/driver), John Booth (driver). Front: Gordon Green (driver), Stan Hepple (driver), Gordon Smith (driver), unknown, Billy Smith (driver) and young Billy Smith aged 2 years.

The annual sports day was a day that everyone looked forward to, especially the wives and children of the staff of the Corporation. Time for a good natter for the women and exciting times for the children. With plenty of competitions, there were many opportunities to win prizes. One such event, the Bonny Baby Competition, was to provide the Corporation with their Chief Payroll Officer. Frankie Briggs, driver, and his wife Ada, entered their 2 year old girl Susan, and, little Susan was to win her section. 13 years later Susan started working in the wages office of the Corporation, and today, she is still working for their successors after 29 years, but now she is known as Mrs Susan Kirtley. Frankie Briggs began working as a conductor in 1950, and he eventually became a tram driver, and then a bus driver when the trams disappeared in 1954. In 1978 Frankie's health took a turn for the worse, and he reluctantly retired. He still gets around and still keeps in touch with the friends he met on the job.

The Corporation also provided the staff with the opportunity to visit the Motor Show, which was held either in London or Birmingham. The competition was that any idea put forward, and was to prove a benefit to the Corporation, the innovator would be invited to the Show.

Susan Briggs winner of the Bonny Baby Competition in 1958.

Frankie Briggs, tram driver 1950-1978 and daughter Susan Kirtley née Briggs 1972-today Chief Payroll Officer.

A trip to the Motor Show, 29th September 1956. Left to right: Geoff Merrick (conductor), Harry Heslop (inspector), Harry Freeman (driver), Margaret Strong (conductor), Bob Reed (engineer foreman), R.T. Tuddenhan (apprentice fitter), Chas Tobitt (driver) and Jack Roberts (chief inspector).

Fred Smith
Driver
1946-1979

John Walton
Driver
1959-1986

Kenny Samuel
Driver
1957-1986

Albert Whisker
Conductor/Driver
1957-1980

John Scott
Conductor/Driver
1966-2000

A. Deogivanni
Driver
1971-Today

Arthur Makel
Driver
1970s

Micky Owens
Conductor
1961-1986

Jock Ewen
Conductor
1950s-1986

Alan Johnson
Conductor
1950s-1986

Part of the entertainment was to be provided by the Corporation Band, a section that was to give exhibitions and performances all over England. Names like Albert Maxsted, Albert Whisker, and for many years, the band leader, Tommy Bryce. Tommy was bandmaster from 1928 until his retirement from the Corporation on 1st November 1960, as an electrician's labourer. The band section had been performing since 1913, with Tommy's father being instrumental in starting the section. As well as Tommy's brother, who emigrated to Australia in 1923, his son, William, and his two grandsons, Brian and Alan, were also members of the band. Possibly the best years in regard to competitions that the band had, was the immediate post-war years, when they won a number of the Durham Brass Band trophies. The Midgley, Thornley and Dainty Dinah trophies, were won under the swinging baton of Tommy Bryce, who also performed for the Palace Orchestra, from 1923 to 1928.

Coupled with the sporting functions, and possibly through the meeting of the wives, other functions were to be arranged. Dinner dances and charity dinners, and, after the introduction of the Safety Awards with the help of R.o.S.P.A., Royal Society for the Prevention of Accidents, the Awards Dinners. Long Service Awards were also well attended, and Branch Fund, and Institute Dinners, and just purely a social, and, quiet night out which workmates and their partners could enjoy.

Once again many names come forward, men and women, who went out of their way, to arrange these functions, so that everyone had the choice of how and where they could be entertained. Ernie Quinn, Stan Finkle, Stan Hepple, Danny Hunter, little Jackie Thompson, Billy Bell, Norman Burlison, Tommy Derivan, Geordie Taylor, Eleanor Brannigan, I could go on forever, Les Robinson, even Alan Wright the Manager got deeply involved. In later years, the early '70s, people like Jimmy Smurthwaite, the Appleby brothers, George and Ritchie, Billy Tarvit, and, so many many others. One such group of people even set up a very

Sunderland Corporation Band.

Chief Inspector Ernie Pullan's retirement. Left to right: Belle Dukes (conductress), Betty Derivan (conductress), Allan Wright (manager), Martha Naisbett (conductress), Violet Buddle (conductress), Brenda Johnson (conductress), Doris Trotter (conductress), Hazel Hardy (conductress), Betty Snowdon (conductress), Pat Entwhistle (driver), Minnie Thompson (conductress) and in front Ernie Pullan.

A quiet night in the Transport Club. Left to right: Doug Watson (tram conductor/driver/bus driver) 1950-1979, Mrs Evelyn Watson, Mrs Agnes Gardner, Tommy Gardner (tram conductor/driver/bus driver) 1951-1979.

A cheque for the Mayor. Left to right: Nicky Carter (driving instructor), Tommy Derivan (driver), Austin Robson (driver), the Mayor, Harry Hughes (conductor), Joe Metcalfe (driver), Deputy Mayor, Bobby Nash (driver), 'Taxi' Young (driver), Alan Wright (manager) and Ken Duncan (personnel officer).

Norman Farrow
Driver/Inspector
1952-1986

Kenny Blackband
Driver/Inspector
1957-1986

successful mime group, called The Twiggs, who gave us all a good laugh at various function, especially around Christmas time. The Twiggs also performed for various charities and to be able to do so, they arranged all of their own change of duties, or days off. Stevie Cowe was the originator of the group, and by the size of him, he was the undisputed manager. From little acorns, a disco group Sweet Charity

George Spoors
Operations Supervisor
1950-1984

Joe Chick
Driver/Instructor
1960-1986

Kitty Robinson née Dee (conductress) 1952-1968.

Les Robinson (conductor/driver) Sept 1946-July 1978.

arose, and also carried out shows for charity, once again raising quite large sums of cash.

Many of the special functions and social evenings would be spent in the Transport Club, in North Bridge Street, near the Wheatsheaf Depot. Stan Hepple, Tommy Derivan, Danny Hunter, Ernie Quin and Tommy Agnew, all spring to mind, and many others. Les Robinson and his wife, Kitty, and their family were frequent visitors to the club, and Brian Robinson and his wife Julie, became very good family friends of mine.

It was still the time when the majority of the staff could communicate with the passengers, joke with them, help mothers with their pushchairs, and be of a friendly nature in general. One particular incident comes to mind

Brian Robinson (conductor/ driver) 1966-1975 and wife Julie.

Don Fletcher
Driver/Instructor
1960s-1980s

Tom Cunningham
Driver/Instructor
1950s-1980s

John Robson
Driver/Inspector
1960s-1990s

Arthur Swinburn
Driver
1950s-1970s

Safety Awards at Pyrex Club 13th April 1985. Left to right: Joe Chick (driver/inspector), Billy Smith (conductor/driver), Tommy Fielding (conductor/driver), Les Watt (conductor/ driver), Freddie Gibbons (conductor/driver), John Walton (driver) behind, David Howard (Director General P.T.E.), Arthur Priest (conductor/driver) and Ces Brown (conductor/ driver).

Joe Gowland
Tram Driver
1920s-1960s

Bob Nesbitt
Inspector
1940s

involving a driver, Eddie Quinnan, and a conductor, Geoff Parks, and some lost property. The Crowtree Road bus station was also the staff canteen and the main change over points for drivers from the Hylton Road Depot. At the time in the 1970s all the bus services through the bus station were very busy and heavy with passenger traffic, and on of the busiest was the Farringdon route, service 2 and 3. It was around 2.30 pm, time for Eddie to take over on Farringdon, and having earlier found a white stick, used by a blind person, Eddie and Geoff decided to play a prank one the large queue of passengers that were waiting for Eddie's bus. Eddie put on a dark pair of glasses and extended the white stick while Geoff kindly guided him down the stairs, out of the canteen, and into the bus station toward the Farringdon stop. Passing the intending the passengers they struck up a conversation, loud enough for the passengers to hear, the conversation went as follows. Eddie, 'Now make sure you come back for me when I'm due off.' Geoff, 'Are you sure you still know where all the controls are?' Eddie boarded the bus, with the help of Geoff and proceeded to feel for the controls. Geoff, 'Have you taken your last lot of nerve tablets?' 'Yes' said Eddie. 'O.K. then I'll be back for you when you're due off.' 'Thanks Geoff see you later.' Well a lot of the staff could observe what was taking place from the canteen windows and we could not believe what was to take place next. Some of the passengers who were unsure, or could not believe what they had seen and heard, quiet rightly stepped back and refused to board the bus, but more surprisingly, the greater number boarded and paid their fares and sat down as normal. Although there was a look of concern on their faces. Of course Eddie let the prank run as far as he could and then informed the rest of the standing passengers that it was a prank, and everyone boarded the bus, while all of the staff were crying with laughing, and lots of passengers were having a good laugh too.

Eddie Quinnan had a number of nicknames, one of which he deserved – Mr Memory Man. He really did have a vast knowledge of sport, and mostly of his favourite, football. While his knowledge was mostly of professional football, his love and passion for the amateur game was just as keen. This

Safety Awards. Left to right: Ronnie Sheraton (driver), Sammy Burgess (driver), Elijah Evens (driver/inspector), The Mayor, Allan Wright (manager), Violet Buddle (conductress), Les Watt (conductor/driver), Joe Metcalfe (driver), The Mayoress, Brenda Johnston (conductress), Harry Wallace (driver), Frankie Briggs (tram/bus driver), 'Taxi' Young (driver), Harry Hughes (conductor), Ossie Watson (driver) and Alan Grundy (driver).

Left to right: Richard Appleby his wife Jenny, Maureen and husband George Appleby.

Queen's Award, 7th September 1977. Left to right: Richard Clements (driver, South Shields), Rene Little (receptionist, Sunderland) and Mr Ron McLean (engineer, Sunderland).

keenness was to give Eddie one of his other nicknames. The Corporation football team was playing probably some of its best football and Eddie, along with many other keen supporters, was following every game that the team played. In a game against South Shields Corporation, in the Cadwallder Cup competition, the transport national trophy, as well as both teams Eddie and other supporters were waiting for a hot meal which was supplied at all national venues. The seating arrangements were very tight and so many of the supporters were sitting with their backs against the wall and could only be served from the other side of the table, over the heads of the other supporters. Although Eddie wasn't very old, the hair on his head was rather sparse, and he was sitting facing the wall, and so the waitress would

Terry Derivan (Sunderland manager).

have to pass the meal over Eddie. Well the meal was beef and gravy, with the usual vegetables. As the meal was being passed to the person opposite Eddie, the waiter, quite accidentally, tipped up the plate which was in her hand and the gravy spilled of the plate onto Eddie's head. It ran down his face, over his new suit, and on to his shoes. One of the popular television adverts at the time was for Oxo gravy. Poor Eddie, from that day he was given the name of Oxo and even when he would pass you on the road, all the drivers would give the gesture of fore finger and thumb flicking together, as though sprinkling gravy salt or Oxo. Eddie got married a short time after this incident to a lady a little younger than himself, but he was such a good man he could do that, and attract younger people with his personality. Sadly for Eddie and his wife it was to be a short marriage, as Eddie was to pass away soon after. If there can be any comfort from this fact, then that could be that Eddie passed away while watching his favourite sports programme on television, and that was Grandstand.

The Twiggs, 1972. Left to right: Alan Hooks, David Jarvis, Eric Cook, Stevie Cow, Ray Wilkinson, Robin Wilkinson and Master Wilkinson.

Why do we call Oliver Parnaby, Charlie? Well when Oliver was a young apprentice engine fitter he was employed by Youngs Garage in Harbour View, Sunderland. When needing to carry out specialist tasks where special tools were required, Oliver had to go to the tool store and withdraw the tool he needed. Youngs Garage was a proficient garage and so the engineers were only able to withdraw tools if they carried out procedure, and to do this the engineers were issued with brass discs with their own name on. Hand in one disc, withdraw the tool, hand in tool and get back your disc. Just before Oliver began working for Youngs, old Charlie had retired and handed in his discs, the foreman, always on the look out to save money, gave Charlie's discs to Oliver and told Oliver it would be only for a couple of weeks. Oliver kept the discs and the name Charlie, and he is still known as Charlie today.

Alf Bradwell
Inspector
1946-1973

Spen Bradwell
Inspector
1946-1976

David Gowland
Inspector
1971-1996

Andrew Johnston
Driver
1959-1990

George Robson
Driver
1971-1995

Adrian Fairless
Inspector
1964-1997

George Potts
Engineer
1956-1986

Freddie White
Driver
1966-1986

Eric Cook
Driver
1971-1994

Billy Maudgham
Driver/Depot
1941-1980

How the stablemen, horse keepers and engineers in the early days of the Tramways Company operated has already been documented and commented on in this book. Many names and characters were also mentioned, sometimes with good thoughts in mind, and, sometimes not so good. In a purely friendly way, on behalf of the drivers and conductors, I would like to make an observation in comparison to the horses in the stables and the horses under the bonnet. Readers may recall the incidents with the horses needing to be changed because of injuries. After being taken to the stables to be changed for a fresh horse, as soon as the next injured horse needed to be changed, then the first horse was used to do the change and the stable boy was fined for using an injured horse for the change. Well, although it was never proved, many situations of a similar nature appeared to happen with the horses were under the bonnet. Buses, double or single, after developing a mechanical fault would be taken to the depot to be replaced by another bus, and when another bus needed to be changed the first bus would be … well like I said it was never proved, but the comparison had to be made. I hope that the engineers that I had, and still have a good relationship with, take the previous comments in the spirit in which they were intended. It is not meant to cast any doubts upon their ability to carry out their engineering duties. It is a well known and documented fact that the Corporation's engineering department staff were the best in the country and maintained all of the vehicles to the highest of standards. On Certificates of Fitness, M.O.Ts, on many occasions the pass marks were 100%. That fact alone speaks volumes for the skills of the engineers.

Hylton Road Depot being demolished 5th September 1987.

Wheatsheaf Depot ready for demolition in 1986.

In the 1950s and '60s and on through to the modern day the General Managers of the Corporation were also the Engineers, men like Harry Snowball, Norman Morton and of course Mr A.H. Wright. All good men but, without the people working under them, it would have been much harder to maintain the high standards already mentioned. Moir Lockhead, is now Chief Executive of First Bus and Neil Scales is now Director General of Manchester Transport, both excellent engineers. Closer to home was Ronnie McLean, who became depot engineer of Sunderland, Tommy Williamson, foreman, but, other than Mr Wright, the engineer who I had most dealings with was George Garrett. I met George and Doug Summerside, while we were serving in the R.E.M.E in Taunton in Somerset. George and Doug were national service men and I was a regular soldier. An interesting story regarding the two conscripts, was that in 1962 just before a football final in which George was playing, they were both given the news that they would have to serve an extra six months at the end of their service. The team lost the final by an own goal, scored by George Garrett. Two days later they found out that they would both be released on time.

The family connections in the traffic side, was also there in the engineering. George Garrett Snr was a tram driver and a bus driver, and probably the influence for George Jnr starting his apprenticeship with the Corporation. George Jnr became manager of Sunderland, and as engineering union shop steward, I began a good and friendly relationship with him. We still keep in touch and pass on all of the gossip. The present depot engineer, Kevin Taylor, also began his apprenticeship, probably because of his father, George Taylor, a bus driver. George was very much involved with the welfare side and was influential in organising many of the social functions. Kevin's mum, Ellen, was also employed for a short while in the depot, and so continued the unique

George Taylor, conductor/driver.

Ellen Taylor née Stoneley, conductress 1940-1968.

Kevin Taylor, Depot Engineering Manager, Sunderland.

family traditions. Kevin, because of his skill as an engineer, and his ability to organise, was sent all over the divisions. Hylton Road, Fulwell Depot, South Shields and the Northern depots in Newcastle, but he was happiest only at the Wheatsheaf Depot and that is where he is today. Stan Rackstraw, foreman electrician, was also carrying on the family traditions by following his father, Bob, an inspector on the traffic side. Stan's son, Peter would also come to work at the Wheatsheaf, but at a much later date.

It would be remiss of me not to mention the other skilled personnel in engineering, other than the management. Mechanics, electricians, trimmers, coachbuilders, welders and fitters, all who contributed, not only in their official capacities, but also in some of their voluntary work. The trimmers and painters, like Geordie Hall and Gary Baker and others. Steve Docherty and Grahame Gibbon, the two supervisors, who transformed ordinary buses into play buses for local children, converted buses into exhibition buses for various companies like the G.M.B Union, Sunderland Football Club (The Roker Rover) and many, many others, all of which they should feel justly proud. Clive Fallon, fitter, who gives quite a lot of his own time, as well as the company's, to the local Lifeboat, of which he is now coxswain.

Many people will remember their days working for the Tramways, and later the Corporation, with many different emotions, some good and some not so good. However, I think that those of the staff who met and married each other will remember only good times, but possibly not all, so I will mention only the happy ones. Jacky Hedley and his wife Doris were certainly happy, Vera and Chris Bell, Stan and Doreen Hepple, and of course I can go on. Jacky Hutchinson and his wife Mary, Ernie Quin and Mary and many, many others, once again too numerous to mention.

There are two marriages of which I would like to specifically expand upon, one from far off and the other

George Garrett, Engineering Manager.

Bob Rackstraw, driver/ inspector, 1920-1962.

A young Stan Rackstraw foreman coach builder.

Margaret Barrow
Conductress
1948-1957

Geordie Pescod
Conductor
1961-1986

Peter Allin
Conductor
1967-1978

Billy Middlewood
Conductor
1940s-1970s

George Wilson
The Last Conductor
1965-2000

Charlie Young
Inspector
1947-1987

Brian Bellamy
Engineer
1966-1998

Hannah Garland
Canteen
1960s-1980s

Kenny Cheal
Inspector
1962-1975

A. McDougal
Conductor
1940s-1970

Wheatsheaf Depot engineers and handymen, 1956. Back row, left to right: George Eales, J. Gardner, T. Wright, H. Kilner, N. Powell, J. Flowers. Front: J. Laws and Eddie Pratt.

closer to home. The bride from afar Roma Kowald, married Tony Paterson, on 11th June 1962, in St Timothy's Lutheran Church, Sunderland, the first couple to marry in that church. Tony met Roma, a district nurse in her hometown of Toowoomba in Queensland, Australia, while he was working with a team of railway workers. Tony was staying with his cousin Alan Paterson, who had immigrated to Australia 8 years before. When Tony returned to England, Roma realised that love had blossomed and followed Tony in February 1962. She then joined Tony, who was already working for the Corporation, as a conductress. Roma's accent was cause for concern when collecting fares, many thought she was from London, but she just laughed at the thought of all the sunshine she had left behind, and that hopefully, very soon, would be returning to. Roma and Tony Paterson did return to Australia in October of 1963 after saving every penny for their return fare from working hard for the Corporation. They still live there, happily, and are visited often by Tony's brother Michael.

Mr and Mrs J.J. Hutchinson – Mary Hutchinson née Mulldoon.

Joe Walton and his wife Vicky were married for 32 years. Who was Joe Walton? and who was Vicky? Well Joe was the Corporation's telephonist from 1958 until 1978. Joe was a conductor for the Corporation before the Second World War, when he joined the Durham Light Infantry, serving in the Far East, he was taken prisoner and remained so for four long years. Upon his return, Joe had not realised that he had contracted a disease, and sadly in 1949, disaster struck. Joe awoke suddenly one morning and, without any warning, he had been struck blind. That was when Vicky became strong for both of them, she cared for and, guided Joe throughout his ordeal, pushing him gently toward fending for himself, and eventually getting work in London as a telephonist. In 1958 they returned, with their five children, to Sunderland, and then on to work again for the Corporation. Their ordeal and the way they both met it head on, shows what a good and strong marriage can do whatever the adversity.

Roma and Anthony Paterson.

Vicky and Joe Walton, conductor/telephonist/receptionist 1930s-1978.

Fulwell Depot Cleaners taking a tea break, left to right, seated Gerry Dawson (driver/instructor), standing Tommy Holmes, standing far right Billy Rowe.

Gibson Crombie, conductor/driver 1967-1986. Gibson was known as the 'Gentle Giant'.

Well it is almost time for the next bus to arrive, but before it does, my final thought I will leave to a young man who passed away a short time ago. Although he never worked in the Corporation days, he came shortly after, and found his place in the hearts and minds of many of the staff. Jimmy Mardghum was what can only be described as a bit of a lad, full of life, mischievous, in a light-hearted way, mad on all kinds of sport – football, cricket, darts – but most of all, he loved his family life.

His wife Colleen and children Lindsey, Natalie and Craig were always uppermost in his mind, and he lived and worked for them. I don't think that a lot of us realised that Jimmy was as ill as we thought, and because he hid his pain so well, with his happy go lucky outlook, we unwittingly encouraged him to do things which he enjoyed, but should not have been doing. Jimmy was ill for some time and went through a number of operations on his stomach, but he eventually succumbed and with great dignity passed away on 15th January 2000, he will be forever remembered and missed by all.

Left to right: Inspector George Mapstone, Inspector Billy Robb, Inspector Blanche Bell in St Thomas's School, circa 1966.

IN MEMORY OF JIMMY MARDGHUM
By Tommy Garner
Bus drivers come and bus drivers go
Jimmy Mardghum was there forever
Sadly we lay him down to rest
In a land called Never-Never
Always smiling so beguiling
That was our boy Jim
Perchance to meet him in the street
Always happy, Never sad
To me he was a bit of a lad
A little joke, so full of zest
They always say God takes the best
This is how I think of him
A lovely lad was this boy Jim
Not much time to say goodbye
From a new bus station in the sky
But he'll be on the number 7
A single ticket – destination heaven
Oft time young Jim, I'll think of you
Time now to say a fond adieu
These flowers I send, not a lot
I've changed their name
I'll forget you not

Retiring today in 1977 with over 400 years service, left to right: Oliver 'Charlie' Parnaby (driver), Jacky Hedley (conductor), John Adamson (depot), Robert Anderson (driver), John Robson (driver) and Stan Thornley (driver).

Wheatsheaf Canteen break time, left to right: Minnie Thompson (conductress), Violet Buddles (conductress), Ronnie Dennis (conductor/depot), George Taylor (driver and canteen representative) and the Mayor of Sunderland.

Hello, is this a bus, no it's two buses, oh no, it's three buses, but they are all full. I may as well have walked in the first place. Still I have enjoyed the journey into the past and the fact that I have been able to reminisce with a few friends. I hope that the readers will have enjoyed the journey too.